Decorative Painting

A Classic Collection

EDITED BY
KATHRYN KIPP
& JENNIFER
LONG

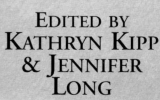

NORTH LIGHT BOOKS
CINCINNATI, OHIO

About the Editors

Kathryn Kipp is the acquisition editor for North Light's decorative painting and home decorating books. Since 1990 she has edited over sixty art instruction books, including *The Best of Flower Painting* (1997). A graduate of the University of Cincinnati, she resides in her hometown of Cincinnati, Ohio. ❦

Jennifer Long is an editor for North Light's decorative painting and home decorating books. She received her bachelor of fine arts from Bowling Green State University. In her spare time, she paints in acrylics and watercolors. She lives in Cincinnati, Ohio. ❦

Other fine North Light Books are available from your local bookstore, art supply store or direct from the publisher.

03 02 01 00 99   5 4 3 2 1

Library of Congress Cataloging-in-Publication Data

Decorative painting : a classic collection / edited by Kathryn Kipp and Jennifer Long.— 1st ed.
    p.   cm.
  Includes index.
  ISBN 0-89134-981-2 (pbk. : alk. paper)
  1. Painting. 2. Decoration and ornament. 3. Flowers in art. 4. Plants in art. I. Kipp, Kathryn. II. Long, Jennifer.
TT385.D437   1999
745.7'23—dc21
                    98-53459
                    CIP

Editors: Kathryn Kipp and Jennifer Long
Production editor: Nicole R. Klungle
Designer: Angela Lennert Wilcox
Cover designer: Mary Barnes Clark
Production coordinator: Kristen D. Heller

Credits

All illustrations for *A Touch of Springtime Elegance*, pages 4-17, © Aileen L. Bratton, CDA.
All illustrations for *Spring Trio*, pages 18-37, © Gretchen Cagle, CDA.
All illustrations for *Keepsake Chest*, pages 38-51, © Ginger Edwards.
All illustrations for *Peaches A-plenty*, pages 52-63, © Deanne Fortnam, MDA.
All illustrations for *Time to Paint Roses*, pages 64-75, © Priscilla Hauser, MDA.
All illustrations for *Blue Iris*, pages 76-83, © Louise Jackson, MDA.
All illustrations for *House Sparrow and Hollyhocks*, pages 84-97, © Sherry C. Nelson, MDA.
All illustrations for *Michelle's Rose*, pages 98-111, © Jackie O'Keefe.
All illustrations for *Filete and Fruit*, pages 112-133, © Jackie Shaw.
All illustrations for *Plums*, pages 134-143, © Donna Bryant Waterson.

Table of Contents

Aileen L. Bratton, CDA

A TOUCH OF SPRINGTIME ELEGANCE

The inspiration for this project came to me while I was in Washington, DC in April. The flowers—tulips, azaleas, daffodils and cherry blossoms—were bursting forth with the birth of spring. Seeing this awakening of nature always makes me want to find time to paint.

I have painted this design on an em-bossed porcelain insert that fits into the lid of a beautiful wooden box. This box would hold many lovely treasures, enhancing a dressing table or any special area.

I hope you will enjoy painting this project as much as I enjoyed designing it. For me, painting always brings joy, happiness and appreciation for the work of God in creating the beauty of this world. ❦

Materials

- 13" × 10" × ¾" (33cm × 25.4cm × 1.9cm) wooden box with 9¼" × 6½" (23.5cm × 16.5cm) porcelain insert available from A Touch of Class by Aileen, 11215 Inverness Ct. NE, Albuquerque, NM 87111; (505) 298-2222 or (505) 298-1144; fax (505) 298-2121

- Rembrandt oil paint in Burnt Carmine (BC)

- Delta Ceramcoat acrylic paint in Light Sage

- Liquitex acrylic paint in Red Oxide

- Winsor & Newton oil paints
  Oxide of Chromium (OC)
  Cadmium Green Pale (CGP)
  Bright Red (BR)
  Naples Yellow Light (NYL)

- Winsor & Newton alkyd paints
  Alizarin Crimson (AC)
  Naples Yellow Hue (NYH)
  Yellow Ochre (YO)
  Burnt Umber (BU)
  Cadmium Lemon (CL)
  Ivory Black (Blk)
  Payne's Gray (PG)
  French Ultramarine (FU)
  Titanium White (W)

- Krylon Matte Finish #1311

- Krylon Crystal Clear Acrylic Coating #1303

- Krylon Satin Finish Varnish #7002

- Winsor & Newton brushes
  series 710 nos. 0, 2, 4 and 6 flats
  series 3A no. 1 liner
  series 995 1-inch (2.5cm) and ½-inch (1.3cm) flats

- Loew-Cornell series 275 ¾-inch (1.9cm) oval mop brush

- 150- and 400-grit sandpaper

- Designs From the Heart Wood Sealer

- Houston Art & Frame, Inc. silver leaf

- Houston Art & Frame, Inc. gold leaf adhesive size

- scraps of velvet fabric, old nylons or cotton balls

- tack cloth

- graphite paper

- tracing paper

- fine-point pen

- stylus

- parchment palette

- Winsor & Newton Artwipes

- Winsor & Newton Sansodor paint thinner

- Winsor & Newton Blending & Glazing Medium

- blue shop towels (optional)

- J.W. etc. Right Step Matte Acrylic Varnish (optional)

Color Palette

White Tulip

Base	Shade	Highlight	Tint	When dry, apply AC + BR.	Then AC + BC + BU and softly blend between the two mixtures.
NYL + W	 PG + OC + (FU) + (Blk)	NYL + W − W	 W + Blk		

Pink Tulip

Dark Area	Buff	Light Area	Shade	Highlight	Tint
 AC + BC + BU	 NYH + BR	 NYL + W	 Dark Area Mix + BU + (Blk)	NYL + W − W	 W + Blk

Blossom Center

Base	Shade	Highlight	Tint	Dark Lines	Splotches
 NYH	 AC + BC + BU	CL + W − W	 Blk + W	 AC + BC + BU + (Blk)	Dark Lines Mix − CL + W

Light Blossom

Dark Area	Light Area	Shade	Highlight	Tint
 AC + BC + PG + (FU)	 NYL + W	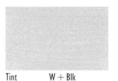 Dark Area Mix + Blk	NYL + W − W	 W + Blk

Dark Blossom

Base	Shade	Highlight	Tint
 AC + BC + BU	 Base Mix + BU − (Blk)	NYL + W − W	 W + Blk − BR + AC

Small Blossom

Base	Shade	Highlight	Dark Lines	Splotches
NYL + W	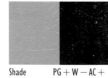 PG + W − AC + BC + Blk	 W + CL	 FU + PG + Blk	CL + W − Dark Lines Mix

Accent Leaves

Dark Area	Light Area	Shade	Highlight	Tint
 AC + BC + Blk	 PG + CL + Blk + W	 Dark Area Mix + Blk	 W + CL − W	 W + (Blk)

Dark Value Leaves

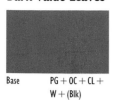 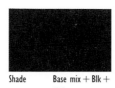 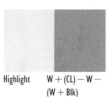 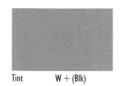

| Base | PG + OC + CL + W + (Blk) | Shade | Base mix + Blk + (FU) | Highlight | W + (CL) − W − (W + Blk) | Tint | W + (Blk) |

Light Value Leaves

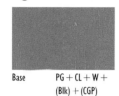 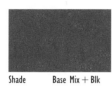 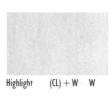 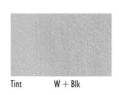

| Base | PG + CL + W + (Blk) + (CGP) | Shade | Base Mix + Blk | Highlight | (CL) + W − W | Tint | W + Blk |

Squiggles and Small Green Leaves
Use Green Leaf Mixtures

---

1 *Prepare the Surface and Transfer the Pattern*
Sand the wooden box with 150-grit sandpaper until the surface and edges are smooth. Remove all the loose sawdust with a tack cloth. Apply Designs From the Heart wood sealer to all areas of the box with a soft, lint-free rag, rubbing the sealer into the grain of the wood. (This sealer dries very quickly.) When dry, use a 1-inch (2.5cm) flat brush to apply Delta Ceramcoat Light Sage acrylic paint to all areas that are not going to be silver-leafed. Paint with the grain of the wood. Allow to dry. If the surface is rough, dip a small piece of 400-grit sandpaper into a small bowl of warm water and dish soap. Lightly sand the surface with the dampened sandpaper. Wipe dry, then apply the second coat of acrylic. When this coat is dry, lightly mist the painted surface with Krylon #1311 matte finish spray.

To prepare the edges for silver-leafing, carefully basecoat them with one coat of Red Oxide acrylic paint. Keep a damp cloth or Artwipe handy to remove paint that might get on the basecoated area. Next, apply the gold leaf adhesive size over the Red Oxide with a ½-inch (1.3cm) flat brush, being certain not to miss any areas. Wash this brush immediately with cold water and soap to remove the sizing. Open the package of silver leaf and remove the string that holds the tissue paper together between the leaves of silver. Cut along the back edge of the package to separate each sheet, leaving the tissue paper dividers in place to protect the leaf. Cut or tear the pieces of silver leaf and tissue into the appropriate sizes to cover the edge of the box. Dampen your fingers and pick up a sheet of tissue-covered silver leaf. Apply the leaf to the edge of the box, then discard the tissue. Each subsequent piece of silver leaf should overlap the previous one. After applying several pieces or covering the entire edge, firmly brush over the leaf with a ¾-inch (1.9cm) mop brush, making certain that the leafing has adhered to the edges. Set the box aside and let dry for about twenty-four hours. (Hope you didn't clean house before you started this project because now you *have* to clean!) After the sizing has dried, burnish with small scraps of velvet, old nylons or cotton balls.

This rubbing action should remove the excess silver leaf so the edges look nice and sharp. If any silver leaf has adhered to the Light Sage background, try to remove it with soap and water, a rag dampened with paint thinner or an Artwipe. Seal the silver leaf by spraying it with Krylon Crystal Clear Acrylic Coating.

Antique the silver leaf with Burnt Umber alkyd paint thinned with a small amount of Blending & Glazing Medium. Apply this mixture to the edges of the box with an old sable brush or lint-free, soft rag. Let it sit for just a few minutes, then remove as much as you desire with a clean, dry, lint-free cloth. Antiquing the silver leaf with Burnt Umber makes it look like pewter.

To prepare the porcelain for painting, wash it with soap and water. When dry, mist the surface with Krylon Matte Finish #1311. Use a fine-point pen to trace the pattern onto tracing paper. Position the tracing on the porcelain insert, secure in two places with masking tape and slide an old piece of graphite paper under the tracing. Go over all the pattern lines with a stylus. Before removing the pattern, lift the graphite paper and check to see that all the pattern lines have been transferred.

Key to Color Mixtures

- In the instructions for this project, a plus sign (+) means to brush-mix the colors listed together. The order of the colors in the color setup indicates the amount of each color used: use more of the first color, less of the second color, etc.

- A dash (-) means to dry wipe your brush and proceed to the next color. Never clean your brush with turp when going from one color to the next. Simply dry wipe and neutralize your brush by loading it with Yellow Ochre or white and then dry-wiping it several times.

- A color in parentheses means that this color is optional. If you use it, do so sparingly. Optional colors give you a way to add variation to all the areas that are being painted with the same colors. ❧

These patterns may be hand-traced or photocopied for personal use only. Above pattern shown full size.

Enlarge at 162% to return to full size.

Enlarge at 162% to return to full size.

2 Rouge Around the Design

The first stages of the rouging are applied before painting the design. Use a very small amount of paint (it may need to be thinned with Blending & Glazing Medium) and a no. 6 flat brush. Load the brush with a mixture of Oxide of Chromium plus Titanium White and place directly on the pattern line above the light blossom. Begin moving the paint outward with light crisscrossing strokes. It may be necessary to pick up a little more Titanium White as you move outward to help fade the color into the background. Repeat this process above the dark blossom. Continue working around the design using the following mixtures: Cadmium Lemon, Titanium White and Naples Yellow Hue or Yellow Ochre; Titanium White and Ivory Black; and Alizarin Crimson, Bright Red, Naples Yellow Hue and touches of Titanium White. Continue until all hard, definite lines between colors are removed and the colors fade into the white background. Also rouge the outside edge of the embossing on the insert, referring to the picture on page 16 for placement. When dry, you may either begin painting the design or you may deepen the rouging colors one more time and fade them out just as you did before. Rouging may remove the graphite lines of the pattern—if this happens, position the pattern over the first application, insert the graphite paper and carefully reapply any missing lines.

Combining Oils and Alkyds

Before you begin to paint the design, I would like to share some tips for painting with a mixed palette of alkyds and oils.

- *When using more alkyds than oils, use more paint and apply with pressure.*

- *When using a complete palette of oils, use less paint and allow the first application of paint to be very choppy and rough, leaving some background visible.*

- *Since the alkyds dry in eighteen hours or less, put out small amounts of paint and change the palette more often than you would with oils.*

- *When the area you're painting or blending becomes tacky and begins to lift, load the brush with fresh paint and apply with pressure to the semidry area. Pressure will push the fresh paint below the semidry surface; using soft "pity-pat" strokes will only lift the paint.*

- *Air movement across the palette or the painting surface will cause the paint to dry more quickly, thus shortening the available blending time.*

- *Oils and alkyds are totally compatible, therefore the same mediums and varnishes may be used with both.* ❦

3 Block In the Design Elements

Make a mixture of Alizarin Crimson, Burnt Carmine, Payne's Gray and a touch of French Ultramarine. This color will be used in the dark areas of the light blossom. I use a technique called brush mixing. Load the brush with the first color listed, then pick up some of the second color and blend these colors together. Then pick up a smaller amount of the third color and blend on the palette. Add a small amount of the fourth color and blend. Edge a no. 4 flat brush into the puddle of paint and pull out a strip, creating your loading area. (Here you will brush-mix the colors listed in the color palettes to create many color variations.) Load the brush using the same amount of pressure you use to apply the paint to the surface. Place this dark-area mixture at the base of the petal under the center of the light blossom and in any shadow areas (areas that are overlapped by another petal). To create a flip on a petal, place the dark-area mixture in the deeper shadow areas under the flip. The outside edge of the dark area, where another color will join it, should be irregular. Refer to the picture above for the placement of the color. (Using color in this manner is called "color side by side" and will create more contrast.) After applying the dark areas, dry wipe the brush (do not rinse the brush—it should still carry some of the dark mixture) and reload with a mixture of Naples Yellow Light plus Titanium White. (Again, you will mix the colors as you load them on the brush.) When applying this color, use short, choppy strokes, allowing the light color to fuzz and blend over the irregular edge of the dark-area mixture.

On the darker blossom, I have used "color on top of color" to create a much darker flower with less contrast. (Color on top of color may also be used to create things that are very light in value.) Load the brush with a mixture of Alizarin Crimson, Burnt Carmine and a small amount of Burnt Umber. Apply with pressure to all the petals. You might want to leave a very small unpainted space between the petals and underneath the flips so you don't loose your pattern.

When you are satisfied with the shading, highlights and tints on the petals, load a no. 2 flat brush with Naples Yellow Hue. Apply with pressure to the blossom centers, creating an irregular outside edge.

Load a no. 4 flat brush with a mixture of Naples Yellow Light and Titanium White. Block in the entire white tulip, really scrubbing over the graphite lines.

I used color side by side on the pink tulip to create more contrast. The dark-area mixture is Alizarin Crimson, Burnt Carmine plus Burnt Umber. Load a no. 2 flat brush with this mixture and apply in the areas indicated in the illustration. The outer edge of the painted area should be left rough so it will be easy to pull the buffing mixture into the dark area—this step will begin the blending. Dry wipe the brush and load with Naples Yellow Hue plus Bright Red. Apply the buffing mixture next to the dark area. The buffing color will form a barrier between the dark and light colors, keeping them from mixing directly and turning muddy. Dry wipe your brush and load with the light-area mixture of Naples Yellow Light plus Titanium White. Block in the remainder of the tulip with this mixture, blending it into the buffing color.

I used a light value of green for the leaves in the higher positions in the design and a darker value of green for the leaves lower in the design. Accent leaves carry the eye around the design. (Accent leaves are usually created with unusual colors, but give sparkle to a painting.) Using a no. 4 flat brush, make a very light green mixture with Payne's Gray, Cadmium Lemon, Titanium White, Ivory Black and a tad of Cadmium Green Pale. Block in the two light value leaves. With a no. 4 flat brush, make a darker green mixture with Payne's Gray, Oxide of Chromium, Cadmium Lemon, Titanium White and Ivory Black. Block in the dark leaf at the back of the design and the base and shadow areas of the tulip leaves. As you pull the dark toward the outer tip of the tulip leaves, lighten the mixture by adding more Cadmium Lemon and Titanium White. On the accent leaves, use color side by side. The dark-area mixture is Alizarin Crimson, Burnt Carmine and a small amount of Ivory Black.

Apply this down the center vein and at the base of the leaf, creating a T shape. Be certain that the outside edge of this area is rough. Dry wipe the brush and load with a light green mixture of Payne's Gray, Cadmium Lemon, Ivory Black and Titanium White. If you get too much Titanium White in this mixture, the leaves will become very muddy. If this happens, add a touch of Cadmium Lemon to clear the color. When applying this light area, pull the mixture into the dark area and begin blending just in the area where the two colors meet.

Load a no. 2 flat with Naples Yellow Light plus Titanium White and block in each petal of the small blossoms by pulling from side to side across the petal. This will give your petals a fatter, fuller feeling. Remove the graphite lines by scrubbing over them as you block in each petal. Load a no. 0 or no. 2 flat with a very light green to block in the small leaves.

4 Shade

If a color break is still visible after adding the light area to the light blossom, dry wipe the brush and then blend by allowing the brush to straddle over the line between the colors. This blending is done with short, choppy strokes, dry wiping often. If the paint begins to lift, use more pressure and load the brush with fresh paint. Blend the dark area into the light area very quickly. The next step is to apply a darker shading color to the overlapped and tucked area, which will give dimension to the blossom. Load a no. 2 flat brush with Alizarin Crimson, Burnt Carmine, Payne's Gray, French Ultramarine and a touch of

Ivory Black. Using pressure, place this color in the areas indicated above.

For the dark blossom, load a no. 2 flat brush with a mixture of Alizarin Crimson, Burnt Carmine, Burnt Umber and Ivory Black and use pressure to place this color in the shadow and overlapping areas. The Alizarin Crimson and Burnt Carmine are very transparent colors and tend to slip and slide. After the petals have been blocked in, let the colors sit for about fifteen minutes before applying the shading colors. Again, let the shading colors sit for a few minutes before you begin to blend them into the base.

To shade the center, load the no. 0 flat brush with Alizarin Crimson, Burnt Carmine and Burnt Umber. Using pressure, apply the shading in a crescent shape to the left side of the center without touching the outside edge of the center.

To shade the white tulip, load a no. 2 or no. 4 flat brush with Payne's Gray, Oxide of Chromium, French Ultramarine and Ivory Black. A tulip petal is painted just like a leaf. The center vein will not be in the exact center of the petal—the light side will cover about two-thirds of the petal, and the dark side will cover about one-third of the petal. On the top or center petal, place a dark triangle of the shading color behind the center vein at the base. Turn the petal so the tip is pointed toward you. Using pressure on the brush, pull the dark shading to form a slight curve that tapers out toward the tip. This dark area has now created a resting area for the center vein. Place the shading color remaining in the brush just above the lower back edge on the light side. If the shading is weak, load the brush again and strengthen the shading. Shade the other petals where they are overlapped by other objects and wherever you wish to create flips. Refer to the picture above for placement of the shading.

The dark and light areas of the pink tulip should be lightly blended into the buffing area. You should see all three of these values (dark, medium and light) when the colors have been connected. To shade the pink tulip, load a no. 2 or no. 4 flat brush with Alizarin Crimson, Burnt Carmine, Burnt Umber and Ivory Black. Place this shading mixture at the base of the tulip, just as you did for the white tulip. You may also refer to the illustration on page 11 for placement of the shading.

To shade the light value leaves, load a no. 2 flat brush with Payne's Gray, Cadmium Lemon, Titanium White and Ivory Black. Place a dark triangle of shading behind the center vein, pulling the color to the outside edge. Turn the leaf so the tip is pointed toward you. With pressure on the brush, pull the shading color to form a curve and then taper it out toward the tip of the leaf. You have now created a resting area for the center vein. The shading always goes behind the curve. Place what shading color remains in the brush just above the lower back edge on the light side. If necessary, this shading may be reinforced with more shading color. A touch of shading may also be added to the outside edge of the light side close to the tip of the leaf.

Using a mixture of Payne's Gray, Oxide of Chromium, Cadmium Lemon, Titanium White, Ivory Black and French Ultramarine, shade the dark leaves as previously instructed for the light value leaves. Refer to the illustration for the placement of the shading.

To blend the accent leaves, place a no. 4 flat brush between the dark and light areas and apply just enough pressure to remove the line of color between the two areas. Load the brush with a shading mixture of Alizarin Crimson, Burnt Carmine and Ivory Black and shade as previously instructed for the light and dark value leaves.

To shade the small blossoms, use a very small brush (such as no. 0 flat) loaded with a mixture of Payne's Gray plus Titanium White, or use Alizarin Crimson, Burnt Carmine and Ivory Black. Use these two different mixtures to break the petals apart and to shade at the base of each petal. Apply with pressure. Refer to the illustration for placement of the shading.

Dry wipe the brush and place a small amount of dark green shading at the base on the dark side of the small leaves. Place a small amount of shading on the light side of the leaves. The shading should just be enough to give a little shape and dimension.

Painting Flips

- The shading does not outline the flips, so when blending, connect the shading and you will have several values within the shadow of the flip. There should always be a strong dark at both ends of the flip.

- The light top edge of the flip must appear to connect to the body of the blossom. To achieve this, load the brush with the light value and place the brush on the edge of the flip. Come up on the chisel edge and pull, connecting the top of the flip to the body of the petal. ❧

5 *Blend the Shading and Add Highlights and Tints*
Dry wipe the no. 4 brush. Begin blending the shading by straddling the line between the shading and the base color of the petal. With pressure on the petal, pull one color into the other. As the line begins to disappear, let up on the pressure and softly blend over the entire petal. Do not make the dark areas all the same value—keep several values within each area. Once the shading has been blended into the petal, it's time to apply the highlights. Load the no. 2 flat brush with Naples Yellow Light and Titanium White and, using pressure, apply to the light areas (the top areas). Highlights lighten and add sparkle to the light area.

Tints are usually placed in the midvalue area or applied from the outside edge. Tints can be used for several reasons: 1) to relate different areas of the design with color; 2) to control the flow of color; 3) to add sparkle to the painting; or 4) to soften an area that is too strong. Cool tints are added to make the area recede into the background.

Add a tint of Titanium White plus Ivory Black to some of the petals of the light blossom. These are applied with very little pressure and are softened over with very light, choppy strokes. Refer to the picture for placement.

After the dark shading has been blended into all the petals, apply the highlights on the dark blossom: Load a no. 2 flat brush with Naples Yellow Light and Titanium White and apply the first stacking of the highlight. Dry wipe and load the brush with a lighter mixture of the Naples Yellow Light plus Titanium White and apply this highlight to all the highlight areas you just created. Build the highlight to a pure Titanium White highlight in some areas.

The first tint applied to the dark blossom is Bright Red plus Alizarin Crimson. Apply these tints as described for the light blossom, referring to the picture for placement. Also apply a Titanium White plus Ivory Black tint to the dark blossom petals.

Stacking the Highlights

I call this technique "stacking the highlights." The highlights are built in layers, with each layer becoming smaller and lighter in value. Apply the highlight with pressure and blend the outside edge with short, choppy strokes. When completed, soften over the entire highlight area. Not all the highlights are built with the same number of layers. By stacking some of the highlights more than others, more value is created within the petal. ❧

Blend the crescent shadow area on the blossom center by applying pressure to the outside edge of the crescent and pulling. It should look splotchy. Using pressure, apply the first highlight of Cadmium Lemon plus Titanium White. Apply a second highlight with a lighter value of the mixture. Apply a pure Titanium White highlight on top. Use pressure to blend the outside edge of the first highlight and then soften over the highlight itself. Add a tint of Titanium White plus Ivory Black on the outside of the center, opposite the highlight in the *center*.

Dry wipe the brush and allow the bristles to straddle over the color break on the white tulip so that the bristles are half on the shading and half on the base color. Blend only where the two colors touch and just enough to break any color delineation. The shading should gradually blend into the base of the tulip, creating a middle value between the two areas.

Now you are ready to apply the highlights to the tulip. Load the no. 2 or no. 4 brush (whichever makes you feel more comfortable) with a mixture of Naples Yellow Light plus Titanium White. You should be using the size of brush that allows you to use the full flat and not just a corner of the brush. Using pressure, apply the highlight at the top of the curve of the center vein. Pull this mixture out in the growth direction of the tulip. Dry wipe the brush, load with a lighter value of the highlight and apply over the top of the first highlight in a smaller area. Dry wipe and load the brush with Titanium White and apply this to the area where the strongest light appears to strike. Apply a smaller highlight on the dark side of the petal, pulling, once again, in the growth direction of the tulip. Stack this highlight with the three values used previously. The other highlights on the petals of the tulip will not be stacked three times. On these, omit the pure Titanium White highlight. Blend these highlights as previously instructed.

The petal is now ready to be cleaned up and refined from the

edges. The tints are added in this step, and lights or darks may be reinforced. Titanium White plus Ivory Black is used for a tint on the shaded side of the center petal tip. Several of the tips of the back petals should also be tinted. This helps make the back petals recede.

Dry wipe the brush and begin to blend the shading on the pink tulip. Refer to the instructions given for blending the shading on the white tulip. Apply the highlights using a mixture of Naples Yellow Light plus Titanium White, then using a lighter value of that same mixture and finally using a small highlight of Titanium White on the center petal. The highlights will not be as strong on the other petals. Dry wipe the brush once again and blend these highlights. Use a mixture of Titanium White and Ivory Black for a tint. These tints should be placed in the same areas as they were previously for the white tulip.

To blend the shading into the light value leaves, dry wipe the brush and place the bristles over the color break, half of the bristles on the shading and half on the base color. Blend only where the two colors touch and only enough to break any color delineation. This should create several values; if you end up with one value, you have overblended. Dry wipe the brush and load with a highlight mixture of Titanium White plus Cadmium Lemon. Highlights are applied using pressure at the top of the curve of the center vein. With each application, the area becomes smaller and the color lighter in value. Apply the first highlight and then break the bottom edge of the highlight by applying pressure and pulling toward the edge of the leaf. Next, a lighter value of the highlight is applied over the first highlight. A third highlight of pure Titanium White may be used depending upon the placement of the leaf in the design. If a third highlight is applied, drop down just a fraction from the center vein area so it is applied in the fullest part of the leaf (where the most light is reflected). Dry wipe the brush and begin the blending process by placing the brush so that half of the bristles are on the back edge of the highlight and half are on the base of the leaf and pull backward toward the base (where the stem comes in) with short, choppy strokes. When this area has been blended, change the direction of blending by pulling at an angle toward the tip of the leaf and blending the bottom edge of the highlight.

The leaf is now ready to be cleaned up and refined from the edges. There are many factors to consider in this step: Tints are added and lights and darks are reinforced at this time. Each leaf always has two things: a dull, reflected light (a cool tint using Titanium White plus Ivory Black) applied on the dark side of the leaf just at an angle from the highlight, and shading that is placed on the outside edge of the light side just under the highlight. The dull reflected light is pulled from the outside edge in, but just a short distance. Blend just enough between the shading and the tint to remove the hard line. To blend the shading placed under the highlight, load the brush with the highlight and softly pull down to soften the dark area. Your final blending strokes should be in the growth direction of the leaf.

Dry wipe your brush and blend the dark value leaves as previously instructed for the light value leaves. The dark areas on the leaf should definitely look darker and also cooler than the light value leaves. Dry wipe again and load with the highlight mixture of Titanium White plus Cadmium Lemon. Using pressure, apply at the top of the curve of the center vein and break the bottom edge of the highlight as instructed for the light value leaves. A second highlight will be applied on all the dark leaves. The tulip leaf on the left side of the design should be highlighted three times, because it is so long that the light strikes very strongly before the tip turns under. The tulip leaf on the right side of the design does not have the center vein developed because the light hits the flip strongly. The middle of the underneath part of the leaf gets a large tint of Titanium White plus Ivory Black. Blend the highlights as previously instructed for the light value leaves. Dry wipe the brush and refine the outside edge of the leaf, applying tints of Titanium White plus Ivory Black as was also previously instructed.

After placing the shading on the accent leaves, dry wipe the brush and soften the shading into the base of the leaves, being careful not to overblend. Dry wipe the brush and apply a highlight of Cadmium Lemon plus Titanium White. Because the colors used on the accent leaves will muddy quickly if too much white is blended over the leaf, use more Cadmium Lemon in these highlights. The highlights are not stacked more than twice because of the placement of the leaves in the design. Apply as previously instructed and then blend. Dry wipe the brush and refine the leaves by pulling the tint (Titanium White plus Ivory Black) from the outside edge. Also reinforce the lights and darks in the leaves as needed for their placement in the design. The final blending on each leaf should be in the growth direction of the leaf.

Using a no. 0 or a no. 2 flat brush, blend the shading into the base of the small blossom. This should be just a pressure stroke or two to soften between the colors. Too much blending will create mud. Dry wipe the brush and load it with a mixture of Titanium White plus Cadmium Lemon. Apply highlights on the petals that should be lifted to the foreground. Build the highlight on some of the petals by adding a touch of pure Titanium White on top of the first highlight. Blend by pressure-stroking between the colors. After highlights are applied and blended, evaluate the petals and, if necessary, add more shading colors to create the depth needed.

The very small green leaves should be just touched with a highlight. Do not overdo these and call too much attention to them.

6 Detail the Painting

I really believe that you shouldn't try to paint any element of the design to a finished stage until you've applied color to all the elements. Then it's time to strengthen the highlights and shading and to determine if the tints help the eye travel through the painting. Evaluate the painting. You may strengthen the highlights, shading, tints and add the details by using one

---

Tips on Glazing

- Make sure the painting is completely dry before glazing.

- To glaze, load a clean brush with Blending & Glazing Medium, blot on a paper towel and apply with very light pressure.

- Apply a small amount of the last color used within the area that you are adjusting.

- Values should get lighter or darker gradually.

- Never use pure white since it is an opaque color and will quickly muddy other colors. ❧

---

of two methods: They may be glazed on with the aid of Blending & Glazing Medium, or they may be applied to a dry surface and softly worked out. I prefer using the wet method.

Glaze stronger darks, highlights and additional tints on the light and dark blossoms if needed. The light blossom should have the strongest highlights of any of the elements. While the glazing is still wet from adding stronger highlights and darks, detail the blossom by adding the dark lines and splotches around the center. Thin the dark line mixture of Alizarin Crimson, Burnt Carmine, Burnt Umber and a touch of Ivory Black with paint thinner. Load a no. 1 liner brush and start to pull the line from under the base of the center of the blossom. Some lines should be longer than others, but they should all follow the curvature of the petal. Using the same mixture and brush, place dark splotches around the center. Some should be larger, some smaller, some farther away from the center, but do not create an obvious ring around the center. Next, dry wipe the brush, load with a thinned mixture of Cadmium Lemon and Titanium White and place light splotches around the center.

Glaze the white tulip, if necessary, adding stronger lights and darks to give the tulip dimension and depth; however, the tulip should not become more prominent than the blossoms. The center vein should be added to the center petals and the side petals where the vein is seen. Use a no. 2 flat brush loaded with a very light mixture of Titanium White plus Naples Yellow Light. With the chisel edge, starting from the base, pull down along the dark side of the vein. If the vein is too prominent, dry wipe the brush and soften. (See tip box on page 17.)

If necessary, glaze the pink tulip to strengthen the lights and darks. While the tulip is damp with Blending & Glazing Medium, apply the center vein as previously instructed for the white tulip.

The light, dark and accent leaves may be glazed to reinforce highlights, shading and tints. When you are satisfied with the painting, the center and secondary veins in the leaves should be applied. Using a no. 2 flat brush loaded with a very light green value, pull from the base down the dark side of the center vein and then turn and pull the secondary veins from the outside edge in. The other side is pulled from the center vein to the

outside. Secondary veins follow the shape of the back edge of the leaf. If veins need to be softened, dry brush them. The veins should appear to go all the way to the edge.

Glaze the small blossoms if necessary. It will be easier to build the darks and the lights using the glazing technique. Apply the dark lines and splotches to the blossoms while they have glazing medium on them. Using a no. 1 liner brush, thin a mixture of French Ultramarine and Payne's Gray plus Ivory Black with paint thinner. Pull the dark lines from the center of the small blossom. Some of the lines should be longer than others. Apply a few small splotches with this dark line mixture. Rinse the brush and load with a mixture of Titanium White and Cadmium Lemon thinned with paint thinner and add a few light splotches, creating the center of the blossom.

If there are hard, definite lines between the different colors originally used to rouge the painting, the rouging may be reinforced at this time by placing Blending & Glazing Medium on the background. Set the porcelain aside and let it dry.

Apply the leaf border design to the sides of the box. Paint the leaves following the instructions for the light value, dark value and accent leaves. Paint the scrolls with a very light green mixture thinned with paint thinner and applied with the no. 1 liner brush. Tint the tips of the scrolls with Alizarin Crimson and Burnt Carmine. Allow this to dry.

When the painting on the porcelain is completely dry, it may be washed with warm water to remove any dust or dirt. Glue the insert to the box with a glue that will firmly adhere porcelain to wood. Varnish the porcelain and the wooden box with Krylon Satin Varnish # 7002, following the instructions on the back of the can. If the painting feels rough after many light coats of varnish, dip 400-grit wet/dry sandpaper into a bowl of warm water and dish soap and lightly sand the surface. Dry and apply several more coats of varnish.

If you aren't comfortable using a spray varnish, varnish the porcelain before gluing it to the box using Right Step Matte Acrylic Varnish. Read the instructions carefully. Apply several very light coats with a good brush such as a 1″ flat brush. After several applications of the varnish, the surface may be lightly wet sanded as previously instructed. I hope you will enjoy and paint in peace and love.

Adding Color to the Tip of the Tulip

The pink color on the tips of the white tulip should be added in step 6. Use a no. 2 flat brush and a very small amount of paint. Place Alizarin Crimson plus Bright Red on the tip and blend into the base. It may be necessary to pick up a small amount of Titanium White plus Naples Yellow Light. Dry wipe the brush and load with a darker mixture of Alizarin Crimson and Burnt Carmine plus Burnt Umber. This is placed over the first mixture but does not cover the first mix and is softened into this pink mixture. Dry wipe the brush and use the chisel edge to work the colors together. This will make the color appear to streak into the petal. ❧

About the Artist

Aileen L. Bratton took her first decorative painting class at the Village Tole House in Arlington, Texas, in February 1970. Her teacher was Bobbye Brown McHugh. Says Aileen, "She was a wonderful teacher and I have been in love with painting ever since that first class." Shortly afterward, Aileen and her family moved back to Albuquerque, New Mexico. Since Aileen didn't have a teacher in New Mexico, she traveled back to Texas for teacher seminars for several years, and she began teaching her own classes in the fall of 1972. "I love teaching and miss having a weekly class and beginning students," says Aileen. "It is so exciting to see new students take the knowledge you give them and fly. I think it rekindles that excitement in me."

Although she no longer teaches weekly classes, Aileen has certainly kept busy: She has published ten books and six instructional videos, has received her Certified Decorative Artist degree and her Master Teacher Floral and has served the Society of Decorative Painters as a committee member, board member and president. Aileen's commitment to decorative painting has earned her the Dedicated Service Award and the President's Commendation Award.

Although she still does some travel-teaching, Aileen is looking forward to having time in the future to paint all the wood she's collected over the years and to create things for her grandchildren to enjoy and treasure. ❧

Gretchen Cagle, CDA

SPRING TRIO

This trio of wooden storage containers has a special flair and panache. Dressed in spring colors and adorned with the flowers of the season, they can be used in a more feminine setting, such as a bath. They are perfect for storing curling irons, blow dryers and all of the other things that quickly accumulate on the countertop.

I used only seven colors to create the designs, making this set of paintings fairly uncomplicated and allowing the design elements to closely harmonize with the background.

One of my favorite techniques for filling a large area with color without painting a lot of design elements is to prepare the background with a bold splash of accent color over a neutral color. The contemporary graphic style of soft lavender applied over the white background immediately draws the viewer's attention. I softened the background colors with quick shots of spray paint, further accenting and softening the design elements. ❧

Materials

- wooden storage containers available from Gretchen Cagle Publications, Inc., P.O. Box 2104, Claremore, OK 74018-2104; (918) 342-1080, fax (918) 341-8909
  tall container: 5½" (14cm) square × 16" (40.6cm) tall
  medium container: 5½" (14cm) square × 12" (30.5cm) tall
  short container: 5½" (14cm) square × 9" (22.9cm) tall

- Delta Ceramcoat acrylic paint in Dusty Plum

- FolkArt acrylic paint in Wicker White

- Winsor & Newton alkyd paints
  Alizarin Crimson
  Cadmium Lemon
  Cadmium Red Deep
  Cobalt Violet Hue
  French Ultramarine
  Ivory Black
  Titanium White

- Krylon interior/exterior spray paint (available at paint and hardware stores)
  Rose #2415
  Flat White #1502

- Winsor & Newton brushes
  Regency Gold series 710 short-bristled, red sable flat brushes, nos. 2 through 8
  series 3A red sable liner brush, no. 0

- poly brush

- Winsor & Newton Blending & Glazing Medium

- gray graphite paper

- stylus

- paper towels

- disposable palette

- Designs From the Heart Wood Sealer

- 400-grit wet/dry sandpaper

- Krylon Satin Finish Varnish #7002

- Krylon Matte Finish #1311

- gold leaf

- gold leaf adhesive

- tracing paper

- odorless thinner/brush cleaner

Color Palette

Poppy Petals

Base	Titanium White + Alizarin Crimson + Cadmium Red Deep	Shade	Shown above. Petal base mixture + Cobalt Violet Hue + Alizarin Crimson + Cadmium Red Deep (this is also the ribbon dark area mixture)
		Highlight	Titanium White

Tint — Shown above. Titanium White + Cobalt Violet Hue + Ivory Black

Streaks — Alizarin Crimson + French Ultramarine + Ivory Black

All Leaves and Stems

Base	Titanium White + Cadmium Lemon + Ivory Black + French Ultramarine
Shade 1	Leaf base mixture + Cobalt Violet Hue

Shade 2 — Shown above. Leaf base mixture + Cadmium Lemon + Ivory Black

Highlight — Titanium White

Tint — Any flower colors

Poppy Center

All Ribbons

Base	Cadmium Lemon + Ivory Black + Titanium White

Shade — Shown above. Center base mixture + Ivory Black

Highlight — Titanium White

Pollen — Ivory Black

Dark Area — Poppy petal shade mixture

Light Area — Shown above. Titanium White + Cobalt Violet Hue + Cadmium Red Deep

Shade — Cobalt Violet Hue + Ivory Black

Highlight — Titanium White

Daisy Center

Base — Shown above. Cadmium Lemon + Titanium White + Ivory Black

Shade — Cobalt Violet Hue + Cadmium Red Deep

Highlight — Titanium White

Pollen Dots — Ivory Black

Ivory Black + Titanium White

Daisies

Undercolor — Ivory Black

Overcolor — Titanium White

Shade — Ivory Black

Highlight — Titanium White

Tint — Cobalt Violet Hue + Ivory Black

Lilacs

Dark Area — Cobalt Violet Hue + Cadmium Red Deep + odorless brush cleaner

Light Area — Titanium White + odorless brush cleaner + Lilac dark area mixture

French Ultramarine + Titanium White + odorless brush cleaner

Lettering

Base — Cobalt Violet Hue + Cadmium Red Deep

Highlight — Titanium White

Poppy

This pattern may be hand-traced or photocopied for personal use only.
Shown full size.

These patterns may be hand-traced or photocopied for personal use only. Enlarge at 131% to return to full size.

1 *Prepare the Surface*

Seal every surface of all three containers with Designs From the Heart wood sealer. Apply the sealer with a paper towel or a poly brush. When dry, sand with the wood grain using 400-grit wet/dry sandpaper. Remove sanding dust with a water-dampened paper towel. Using a poly brush, paint all surfaces with several coats of Wicker White.

Transfer the patterns to tracing paper. Position the appropriate tracing on each container and slip a sheet of gray graphite paper under the pattern. Using a stylus, transfer the ribbon onto each container. Paint the area above the ribbon with Dusty Plum, applying the color with a poly brush. Allow to dry and, if necessary, apply a second application of Dusty Plum. Also paint the routed edge of each lid with Dusty Plum.

When dry, apply a light dusting of Flat White spray paint to the Dusty Plum area of the container. Hold the can of paint about two feet from the surface and apply an extremely light application of color. When finished, the color should just barely be visible, adding a mere accent of white to the plum area. Be sure not to cover too much of the plum color. Don't worry if this color sprays onto the white areas or if it looks slightly splotchy or irregular. This will add to the softness of the color.

Next, add a spray of Rose spray paint along the lower edges of each container. Try to aim the spray so that most of it will fall along the lower left side, just below the ribbon. The color application should be soft, transparent and barely visible. Be sure to add some Rose spray onto the lid and in splotchy areas on the sides of the containers.

Following manufacturer's directions, apply gold leaf to the heart handles on the lids and on the routed edges between each panel on the containers. Allow the surfaces to dry twenty-four hours and then apply a light application of Krylon Matte Finish #1311 to all areas.

Transfer the remainder of the main design elements using gray graphite paper, omitting stems, lilacs, lettering, water drops and pollen dots.

2 Basecoat the Poppy and Leaves

Using a no. 8 flat brush, load with a brush mix of Titanium White plus a small amount of Alizarin Crimson plus a very small amount of Cadmium Red Deep (see the poppy petal base mixture on page 20). Basecoat the entire poppy with a smooth, even application of color. If you run out of color before completing the basecoat, continue to brush mix additional color into the previously mixed color. Don't be concerned that the colors are slightly different. This will add to the natural appearance of the blossom and create variety in the petals. If you can no longer see your pattern lines bleeding through the dry paint, you may wish to place the traced pattern over the design and retrace the petal edges. Drop a small amount of this mixed color onto the poppy buds.

Using the no. 4 flat brush, brush mix Cadmium Lemon plus Ivory Black plus a small amount of Titanium White (see the poppy center base mixture on page 20). Block this color into the poppy center. With a pencil, draw in the center indentation.

Using the no. 4 flat brush, brush mix Titanium White plus Cadmium Lemon plus small amounts of French Ultramarine and Ivory Black (see page 20, leaf base mixture) to make a very pale green. Apply a smooth application of color to each leaf. Apply a bit of the leaf mixture to the green areas of the buds.

3 Shade the Poppy and Leaves and Apply Dark Areas to the Ribbon

Using a no. 6 flat brush, brush mix the shading color. Begin by picking up the poppy base mixture into the brush and then add Cobalt Violet Hue, Alizarin Crimson and a very small amount of Cadmium Red Deep. The shading color should be a deep red-violet, as shown for the poppy shade mix on page 20.

Apply the shading color onto a petal, dry wipe the brush, blend the shading with the base color and then continue to the next petal, completing one petal a time. This way you will be able to adjust colors if necessary. Apply shading next to the flower center, under petal overlaps and within the folds along the petal edges. The strongest shading should fall along the outer edge of the petals, directly behind the folds. The shading is less dominant as it moves along the creased edge of the fold. Be sure to place a small amount of shading on the portion of the fold that is the underside of the flower. When blended, you may find it necessary to apply an additional application of color along the petal edges to increase the intensity or strength of the shading. Be sure that all color is blended so there are no hard breaks of color forming strong lines between the base color and the shading. Dry wipe the brush before continuing to the next step. Apply a small amount of shading along the lower edge of each bud.

Apply shading to the poppy center with a no. 2 flat brush, being sure to dry wipe the brush before blending the color. To create this shading color, add Ivory Black and a small amount of Cadmium Lemon to the poppy center base mixture to make a very dark green (see page 20). Apply the shading along the lower edge of the poppy center and gently soften into the base color. If necessary, re-establish the center indentation. Within the center indentation, apply shading along the right side and barely blend the color within the center. Apply additional shading along the left outside edge of the center indentation and barely blend.

Pick up the leaf shading color in a no. 4 flat brush and apply to each leaf. Some leaves may be shaded with the base mixture plus Cobalt Violet Hue (leaf shading mixture 1 on page 20) and others with the base mixture plus Cadmium Lemon plus a small amount of Ivory Black (leaf shading mixture 2). Apply the shading at the stem end of the leaf and down the center vein area on most leaves. When shading is applied at the center vein area, a strong dark/light separation forms along an arched line. Keep the dark side of the leaf smaller and the light side of the leaf larger. After applying the color, dry wipe the brush and barely blend, without crossing over the dark/light separation line. Shade the lower edge of the green areas on the buds.

Using a no. 2 flat brush loaded with the poppy shading color (see page 20), apply the dark area to the ribbons as shown.

4 *Highlight the Poppy and Leaves and Add Light Areas to the Ribbon*

Highlight all petals with Titanium White, applied with the no. 6 flat brush. Apply the strongest color on the top petal where two petals overlap each other and on the folds. Be careful when applying color so that it does not drag into the dark shading color you applied previously. Apply secondary highlights, which are softer and less intense, along the outer edges of the petals to lift and give dimension to the flower.

After applying each color area, dry wipe the brush and gently and carefully blend into the base color. The base color is now the mid-value area of the design and should act as a buffer between the highlight and shading colors. The highlight color should blend only with the base color, since that is the only color it touches. It should not be applied in such a way that it touches the dark, shaded areas of the design. It is important to remember that each color only blends with the color that it touches. Blending colors beyond this point will result in muddy, overblended colors.

After applying and blending the highlights, strengthen them on the front center petals, making sure that the fold has the strongest highlight. Highlight the tips of each of the buds.

Using the no. 2 flat brush, apply Titanium White highlights to the poppy center. Apply the highlight on the right outside edge of the indentation. Dry wipe the brush and barely blend into the base color. Dry wipe the brush and apply highlights on the left inside of the indentation. Again, dry wipe the brush and barely blend the colors.

Using a no. 4 flat brush, apply a strong Titanium White highlight on the leaf at the center vein area next to the shaded side of the leaf. This will abut the shaded area but will not blend with it. Be sure that the highlight is broad and wide where the leaf is the broadest and that it tapers toward the leaf tip. Do not apply highlight onto the dark area at the stem end. Dry wipe the brush and blend without crossing over the dark/light separation line. On some leaves, you may wish to add a small amount of the highlight color along the

dark, outside edge of the leaf. When blending, be careful that the color does not blend too far into the shaded area. Add just a touch of highlight on the upper edge of the green bud areas.

Using the no. 2 flat brush, paint the light areas of the ribbons using a mixture of Titanium White plus Cobalt Violet Hue plus a very small amount of Cadmium Red Deep (see the ribbon light area mixture on page 20). Dry wipe the brush and blend between the colors.

5 Tint the Poppy and Leaves and Shade the Ribbon

Apply tints to the mid-value areas of the poppy. Brush mix a soft violet using Titanium White plus Cobalt Violet Hue plus a small amount of Ivory Black (see page 20). Load a scant amount of the color onto the no. 6 flat brush and apply to the poppy petal. Dry wipe the brush and blend with a streaky motion, carrying color toward the flower center.

Most of the leaves are tinted with their flower colors. It isn't necessary to tint all leaves—do only a few. Use a no. 4 brush to tint the leaf edge. Dry wipe the brush and barely blend into the leaf.

Deepen a portion of the ribbon dark areas with a mixture of Cobalt Violet Hue plus a small amount of Ivory Black. Using the no. 2 flat brush, tuck a small amount of the color into the overlaps where the ribbon goes behind the leaves, flowers, etc. or where the ribbon narrows to a thin line. Dry wipe the brush and blend to eliminate any harsh color breaks.

6 Finish the Poppy, Leaves and Ribbon

To finish the poppy, strengthen the highlights and add additional shading where necessary. The highlights on the poppy center can be strengthened with Titanium White. When finished, add strong dark streaks on the back center petal and on the front center petal that contains the water drops. For the streak color, brush mix Alizarin Crimson plus small amounts of French Ultramarine and Ivory Black. Using a no. 4 flat brush, apply the color in a tight, concise band deep into the overlaps. Dry wipe the brush and stand it

on the chisel edge, then slightly pull and streak the color into the petals.

Apply pollen dots using the corner of the no. 2 flat. Dip the corner into fresh Ivory Black and pull away a tail of paint. Gently touch only this tail of paint to the poppy surface. Pull the brush away, leaving a crisp dot of color. Pressing so hard that the bristles of the brush touch the surface will result in a dot that may be too large or appear smudged. Most of the dots will fall along the left and right side of the center, with fewer dots above the center. Position just a few dots on the front of the flower center. Position dots above the flower center over the dark streaks so they are barely visible. You may feel more comfortable positioning the pollen dots when the rest of the flower is dry. If you make a mistake, they can easily be removed from the dry surface without damaging the previously completed work.

Vein lines are applied with the chisel edge of a no. 4 flat brush. For a crisp, sharp vein, the brush must have a clean, sharp chisel edge. Brushes with bristles that are worn, separating or fat in appearance will not yield the desired results. Load the brush with the leaf base color (see page 20). Stand the brush on the chisel edge at the stem end and gently pull through the dark area of the leaf. Apply pressure as you begin to pull the vein and let up on the pressure toward the leaf tip. Using the paint that you have picked up on the brush, apply a few side veins, pulling from the center vein toward the outer leaf edge. The center vein should just barely sit inside the dark side and not on the dark/light separation line.

With a no. 2 flat brush, apply Titanium White highlights to the ribbon. Highlight the center of the light areas and in the areas where the ribbon is widest. Dry wipe the brush; blend and soften the color breaks. Next, apply the tapered ends to the ribbon. Load the no. 0 liner brush with thinned color (use the same color that appears on the ends of the ribbon) and pull out a hairline of paint on the tips of the ribbon. Be sure these tapers of color form a very thin line that curls into the design.

Paint all stems with the leaf base colors. Add the water drops as instructed on the next page. Paint the filler lilacs using the instruc-

tions for the lilac design on pages 35–36, keeping the colors red-violet to violet. To flyspeck the surface, make an inky-thin mixture of odorless brush cleaner and Cobalt Violet Hue. Load the color onto a no.

8 flat brush and run your finger across the bristles, allowing flecks of paint to land on the surface. Fleck all areas including the top and side panels. Repeat with a thinned mixture of the poppy petal shade color.

Water Drops

Water drops can be painted while the design elements are still wet, or you may paint them on a dry surface. If painting on a dry surface, apply a thin application of Winsor & Newton Blending & Glazing Medium in the general area of the droplet and then paint the drop into the glazing medium. It will feel like you are painting in wet paint. Water drops should be painted with a no. 2 flat brush with an excellent chisel edge.

1 Create the Shape of the Drop

Load Titanium White onto the flat brush. Stand the brush on the chisel edge along the long side of the drop. Begin to pull downward along the long side, applying almost no pressure on the brush. As the drop fattens, apply pressure, flatten the brush and wrap along the full, fat portion of the drop. As you begin to pull up along the short side of the drop, let up on the pressure and return to the chisel edge of the brush, keeping the drop open at the top. The strongest, boldest application of color should be in the fat portion of the drop. If necessary, apply additional Titanium White in this area.

2 Blend the Interior of the Drop

Dry-wipe the brush and blend inside the droplet, barely softening the Titanium White into the base color or into the Winsor & Newton Blending & Glazing Medium. Keep the upper portion of the drop open with the base color visible.

3 Apply Shadow Areas

Dry-wipe the brush and pick up a color that is a value darker than the base color and apply the shading. Outside the drop, apply the color, beginning at the top of the drop, in the same manner as you applied the Titanium White to form the stroke. Stand the brush on the chisel edge and pull down the exterior of the drop, applying pressure as you wrap around the bottom of the drop. At the bottom, immediately let up on the pressure, returning to the chisel edge and just barely wrapping the color under the drop. Apply just a touch of the same color in the opening of the drop. Dry wipe the brush.

4 Blend the Shadows and Apply Glints

Soften the shadow areas into the base color or medium with the dry-wiped brush. Apply Titanium White glints with the corner of a flat brush or with a liner brush. (If using a liner brush, thin the paint to a flowing consistency with odorless brush cleaner.) On the interior of the short side of the drop, apply a dot and a broken line of color just inside the white area, forming the outer drop shape. Along the bottom right side of the interior of the drop, position a bright white glint in the form of a dot. ❧

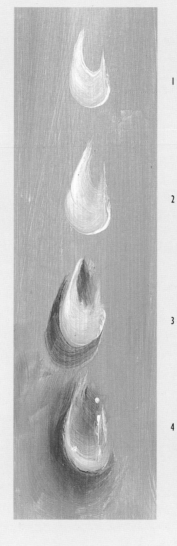
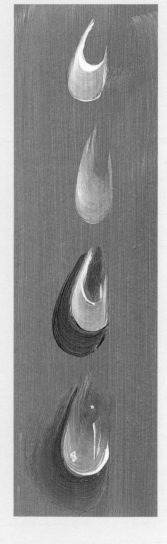

7 Basecoat the Lettering

Using a no. 2 flat brush, basecoat the lettering with a mixture of Cobalt Violet Hue plus a small amount of Cadmium Red Deep. Dry wipe the brush.

8 Highlight the Lettering and Linework

With the no. 2 flat brush, pick up Titanium White and apply to the widest portion of each letter and on any prominent ascenders or descenders. Dry wipe the brush and barely blend to soften. Using the liner brush loaded with thinned base color, extend the tapers onto each of the letters.

When the painting is thoroughly dried, varnish with Krylon Satin Finish Spray Varnish #7002, following the manufacturer's instructions.

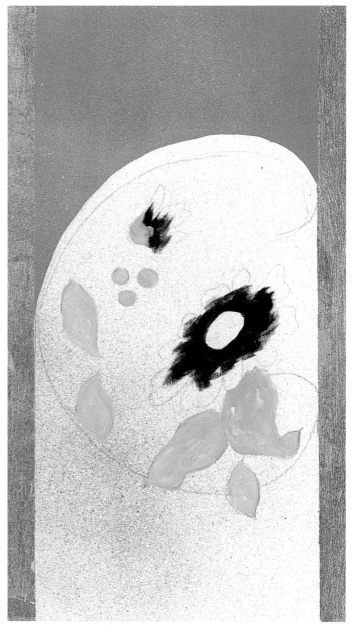

9 *Prepare the Daisy Surface*
Follow the surface preparation instructions on page 23 and transfer the pattern to the surface.

10 *Apply Undercolor to the Daisy Petals*
Using the no. 6 flat brush, apply a collar or halo of Ivory Black around the center of the daisies. Where flower petals are long, the color should extend further into the petals. The edges of the Ivory Black color should be softened and feathered into the petals, leaving no harsh lines of color. Apply a touch of the undercolor along the lower edge of the petals on the daisy bud.

11 *Apply Overcolor to the Daisy Petals and Base Center*
Randomly stroke the petals on using the no. 6 flat brush loaded with Titanium White. Stroke a petal on one side of the flower and then paint a petal in another location until all petals are completed. Random stroking of the petals will allow for a more natural flow to the flower center—when stroking the petals in a sequence, it's very easy to repeat the stroke direction used on the previous petal, causing a pinwheel look to develop.

Most petals are done in two strokes. Position the brush at the tip of a petal and stroke along the left side of the petal, pulling toward the flower center. (If you are left-handed, stroke along the right side of the petal.) Apply slight pressure on the brush as you begin the stroke and let up on the pressure as you taper toward the flower center. Now stroke the other side of the flower petal in the same manner. You may find it easier to stroke this petal if you bring the unfinished side to your left (to your right for left-handers).

Using a no. 4 flat brush, apply a basecoat of brush-mixed Cadmium Lemon plus Titanium White plus a small amount of Ivory Black to the daisy center (see daisy center base on page 20).

Petal Strokes

Don't be alarmed if you get a gap between the strokes, or if they overlap each other, as shown in the left example. The blending process in step twelve will fix any gaps or overlaps.

12 *Blend the Daisy Petals and Add Shading*
Dry wipe the brush and then blend down the center of each flower petal where there are two obvious strokes (see "Petal Strokes" on the previous page). Barely touch at the petal edge and make a very soft, nonpressured stroke toward the flower center. Blend only enough to get rid of the two-stroke look, leaving a strong dark area on each petal at the flower center. Don't be alarmed if there are dark gaps between the petals at the flower center. This will only give additional depth to the flower. Wipe the brush and apply a small amount of Ivory Black shading between overlapping petals so that the underneath petal will be darker in value and appear to recede. If you have obtained good petal separation during the stroking process, there's no need to apply shading in those areas that are already well defined with dark/light separations. Stroke the daisy bud in the same manner.

Using the no. 2 flat brush, brush mix Cobalt Violet Hue and a small amount of Cadmium Red Deep. Apply the color along the lower edge of the daisy center. Dry wipe the brush and blend to soften and merge the colors.

13 *Tint the Daisy Petals and Highlight Center*
Pick up a scant amount of Cobalt Violet Hue plus a very small amount of Ivory Black on a no. 4 flat brush and apply to the tip of the petals. Dry wipe the brush and softly blend the color into the petals. Stroke the bud in the same manner.

Pick up a generous amount of Titanium White on a no. 2 flat brush and tap it onto the top of the daisy center. Keep the color stronger along the top left side and weaker along the right side. If necessary, reapply the highlight to create an intense white color.

14 Finish the Daisy Design

Strengthen the middle area of each petal with Titanium White. Apply the color with the no. 4 flat brush, dry wipe and then gently blend, leaving the darkest color at the flower center and the violet tip. It may be necessary to apply highlights several times in order to obtain an intense, bright highlight.

Apply pollen dots using the corner of the no. 2 flat brush. Dip the corner of the brush into fresh Ivory Black, pulling away a tail of paint on the brush. Gently touch only this tail of paint to the daisy surface. Pull the brush away, leaving a crisp dot of color. Allowing the bristles of the brush to touch the surface will result in a dot that may be too large or smudged-looking. Most of the dots will fall to the left and right of the center along the lower edge, with fewer dots above the center. Apply a few additional dots with Ivory Black plus Titanium White. On the front and sides of the flower center, the dots should fall on the petals and on the flower center. On the back of the center, the dots should fall only on the flower petals. You may feel more comfortable positioning the pollen dots when the flower is dry—if you make a mistake, they can easily be removed from the dry surface without damaging the previously completed work.

Follow the instructions given with the poppy design to paint the leaves, stems, ribbon, water drops and lettering. Paint the filler lilacs using the instructions for the lilac design, keeping the colors red-violet to violet. Following the instructions for the poppy design, flyspeck the surface with an inky-thin mixture of odorless brush cleaner and Cobalt Violet Hue and then with the poppy shade mixture (on page 20). When the painting is thoroughly dry, varnish with Krylon Satin Finish Spray Varnish #7002, following the manufacturer's instructions.

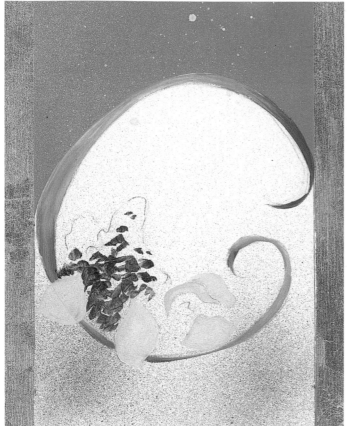

15 *Paint the Dark Areas of the Lilacs*
Follow the surface preparation instructions for the poppies. Transfer the lilac pattern to the surface. Transfer only the leaves and a rough outline for the flower forms. Apply the dark areas with a mixture of Cobalt Violet Hue plus Cadmium Red Deep plus odorless brush cleaner. Keep the strokes compact and dense at the base and less dense as you travel up the flower form (see "General Instructions for Lilacs"). Dry wipe the brush.

Paint the leaves using the colors and techniques described for the poppies.

16 *Apply the Lighter Areas of the Lilacs*
Load the dry-wiped brush into Titanium White plus a bit more odorless brush cleaner and a scant amount of the previously applied darker color remaining on your palette. Apply this mixture toward the tips and outer edges of the applied darker color in the last step. Notice the value changes and the tapering of color that form the lilac tip. Be free and loose with the strokes, allowing the lighter values to soften into and overlap the edges of the darker, previously applied color. Dry wipe the brush.

General Instructions for Lilacs

Lilacs are painted in a very loose, free-flowing form, using color that is thinned to an inky consistency with odorless brush cleaner. Each application of color is applied with a no. 4 or no. 6 flat brush. Load the color onto the brush and then press against the surface, lifting and turning the brush in different directions. You should work off the flat edge as well as the corner of the brush. Each change of brush position will create a different shape.

You may also want to occasionally add a bit more brush cleaner to the mixture to create additional value change—a higher proportion of brush cleaner will create a lighter value of color. Additional value change can be created by adding other colors to the mixture. When applying the initial application of color, start at the base of the flower form and apply closely compacted strokes of color, allowing some background to show through. As you move away from the base of the flower, allow the colors to become lighter in value and less dense so that more of the background color is visible.

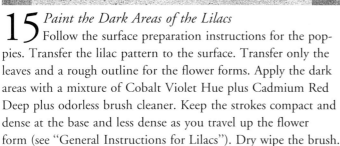

17 *Finish the Lilacs*
With the dry-wiped brush, pick up a small amount of French Ultramarine plus Titanium White and some odorless brush cleaner. Apply the less dominant flower forms along the outer edges of the main cluster. Be sure to keep them very loose and light in value, retaining plenty of visible background. For lighter value flowers, add additional odorless brush cleaner.

Now pick up a bit of the leaf colors and add a few thinned splotches of color, giving the illusion of a few leaves tucked among the flower forms. On the taller stalks, you may wish to add the suggestion of stem lines that are just barely visible through the flowerlets. Use the liner brush to apply these stems. Thin the paint with a bit of odorless brush cleaner to the remaining mixture on the brush.

Paint the ribbon, water droplets and lettering, following the instructions given for the poppies. Flyspeck the surface with a thinned mixture of odorless brush cleaner and Cobalt Violet Hue and then with the poppy shade mixture, as you did with the previous designs. When the painting is thoroughly dry, varnish with Krylon Satin Finish Spray Varnish #7002, following the manufacturer's instructions.

About the Artist

Gretchen Cagle has been painting and teaching decorative painting for twenty-six years. She is a member and past president (1985–1986) of the Society of Decorative Painters and was named a Certified Decorative Artist (CDA) in l977. She was awarded the coveted Dedicated Service Award for her many contributions to the society and to the Decorative Arts Collection. Gretchen is a travel teacher, holding seminars both nationally and internationally. She has authored twenty books and ten videos on decorative painting, which are distributed worldwide. In addition to her teaching career, Gretchen also owns and operates her own publishing company, which publishes and distributes books by forty of the leading authors and painters in the decorative painting industry. ❦

Ginger Edwards

KEEPSAKE CHEST

I enjoy painting, and I especially like to design and paint items that will be useful as well as decorative—this little chest is a perfect example. It can hold silverware, hosiery, hankies or the *TV Guide* and remote, or store mementos of special events in our lives. Instead of stowing items out of sight in closets or drawers, try using painted chests and boxes. They are wonderful accessories and their contents are readily accessible.

I have used several simple techniques in painting this design: paint applied in an opaque manner, paint applied transparently (by adding a small amount of Blending Gel Medium and water) so that the underpainting shows through, and tiny amounts of paint brushed on a dry surface. Each technique yields a different result; combined, they produce an interesting, easy-to-accomplish painting.

The key to successfully painting this design is to allow each step to dry before going on to the next. By allowing the paint to dry between steps, you maintain greater control of your paint and can wipe off any mistakes without fear of ruining previous steps. ❦

Materials

- 11½" × 6½" × 7" (29.2cm × 16.5cm × 17.8cm) wooden chest available from Art Craft Wood, 415 East 7th St., Joplin, MO 64801; (800) 537-2738

- *FolkArt acrylic paints*
Bluebonnet
Burnt Sienna
Burnt Umber
Dioxazine Purple
Dove Grey
Lemonade
Linen
Night Sky
Periwinkle
Pure Gold Metallic
Purple Lilac
Raw Sienna
Sunflower
Wicker White
Wintergreen

- *Bette Byrd Golden Aqua Sable brushes*
series 200 nos. 4, 6, 10 and 12 flats
series 100 no. 2 round
series 400 10/0 liner
series 600 nos. 2 and 4 filberts
series 1000 ¼-inch (.6cm) dagger (similar to a sign painter's brush, but with much shorter bristles)
1-inch (2.5cm) flat

- *tracing paper*

- *stylus*

- *FolkArt Blending Gel Medium*

- *J.W. etc. First Step Wood Sealer*

- *waxed palette*

- *water container*

- *fine-grade sandpaper*

- *graphite paper*

- *tack cloth*

- *clear ruler*

- *masking tape*

- *white chalk pencil or soapstone (used to mark panels on chest; both are water soluble)*

- *small piece of natural sponge (about the size of an egg, with an irregular hole pattern)*

Color Palette

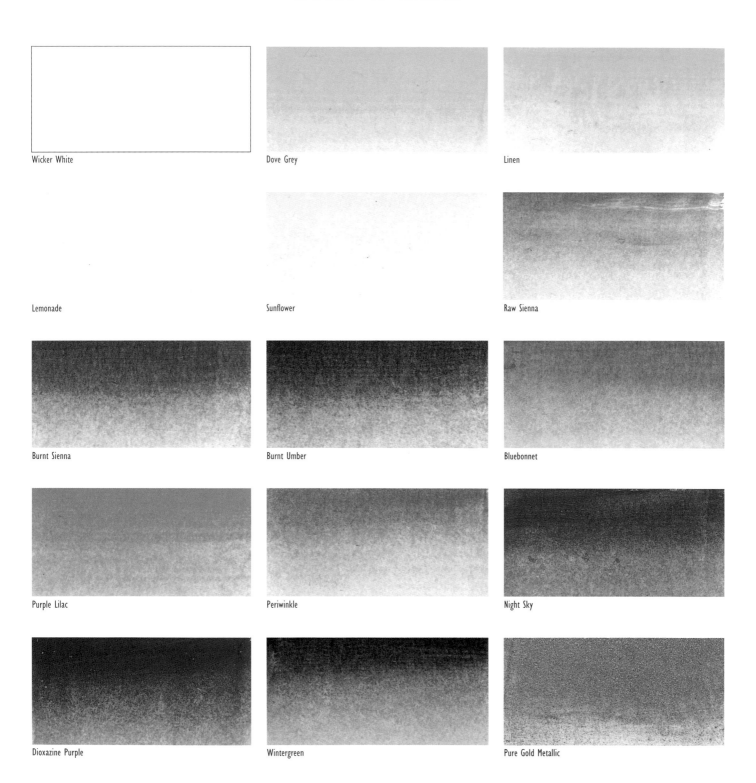

Wicker White

Dove Grey

Linen

Lemonade

Sunflower

Raw Sienna

Burnt Sienna

Burnt Umber

Bluebonnet

Purple Lilac

Periwinkle

Night Sky

Dioxazine Purple

Wintergreen

Pure Gold Metallic

I have painted color swatches using a sideloaded flat brush. As
you can see, the intensity of a color can be altered by the
addition of Blending Gel Medium and/or water.

In addition to the pattern I used on the front of the chest (above), I have included a small pattern that is suitable to paint on the side panels (below). The pattern given is for the left end of the chest. The design should be reversed for the opposite end of the chest. Use the same painting procedure as for the large design.

These patterns may be hand-traced or photocopied for personal use only. They are shown here full size; enlarge or reduce as needed for your project.

1 Prepare the Surface and Establish Design Elements

Basecoat the chest inside and out with a mixture of 1 part First Step Wood Sealer and 3 parts Dove Grey acrylic paint, using a dampened 1-inch (2.5cm) flat brush. Let the paint dry and sand lightly with a fine-grade sandpaper. Wipe the surface with a tack cloth. Apply another coat of the Dove Grey, but this time do not add sealer to the paint.

After the paint is thoroughly dry, position the traced pattern on the surface and tape it into place, then slip a piece of graphite paper under the tracing. Use a stylus to lightly trace over all the lines. Do not transfer the detail (such as the stamen and vein lines).

Use the no. 10 flat brush to basecoat the leaves with Linen. Basecoat the daisy centers with Sunflower, using the no. 6 flat brush. The no. 2 filbert works best to basecoat the violets. Basecoat the upper petals of the violets with Purple Lilac, the side petals with a mixture of equal amounts of Purple Lilac and Periwinkle and the lower large petal with Periwinkle. All basecoats should appear smooth and opaque. If necessary, apply a second coat of paint after the first is dry. Thin Bluebonnet with a small amount of water and Blending Gel Medium and stroke the daisy petals with this transparent paint, using the no. 4 filbert brush. Allow the paint to dry before continuing.

Tip If your transfer paper is new, wipe the excess graphite from the surface of the paper with a soft tissue. This will allow you to avoid difficulty in covering dark pattern lines as you paint. ❧

2 Begin Shading

Lightly moisten a no. 6 flat brush with blending gel medium and water. Sideload the brush by tipping one corner in Burnt Sienna, then stroking the brush on a waxed palette several times to distribute the paint in the bristles. The paint should be intense on one side of the brush, fading away so that the opposite side of the brush has no paint. Shade the daisy centers with the brush positioned so that the Burnt Sienna side is on the edge nearest the petals. After stroking on the paint, it may be necessary to wipe the brush and blend lightly.

Lightly moisten a no. 10 or 12 flat brush and sideload with Wintergreen, just as you did for the Burnt Sienna. Shade the outer edges of the leaves, beginning the stroke at the base of the leaf and pulling toward the tip. Make sure the paint is stroked on the outer edge of the leaf. When one side is shaded, rinse the brush, reload and shade the opposite side of the leaf. Moisten a smaller flat brush, sideload with Wintergreen and shade the stem of the uppermost daisy, as well as the calyx of the violet bud at the lower left of the design.

To shade the daisy petals, lightly moisten a no. 6 or 8 flat brush with Blending Gel Medium and a small amount of water, then sideload with a mixture of equal amounts of Wintergreen and Burnt Umber. Study the illustration and notice that the shading is stroked on each back petal next to the center, while the shading is stroked across the *tips* of the side and front petals. This will create dimension within the daisies even at this early stage.

> ## Tip
> If you're having a difficult time stroking the paint on the dry surface, try moistening the area you're painting *sparingly* with Blending Gel Medium plus a tiny amount of water prior to applying paint. Premoistening with a too-liberal coat of Blending Gel Medium and water will result in paint that will not adhere and difficulty in blending. ❧

3 *Complete the First Shading*

Sideload a lightly moistened no. 10 or 12 flat brush with Wintergreen and stroke the shading at the center vein of the leaves. Position the brush so that the side of the brush holding paint is next to the center vein area. Begin the stroke at the base of the leaf, pulling toward the tip. Lessen the pressure on the brush as you near the tip of the leaf so that the shading decreases in intensity. Where two leaves overlap, the shading should be applied to the underneath leaf in order to separate the two leaves.

Begin defining the violets by sideloading a no. 4 or 6 flat brush with a mixture of equal amounts of Night Sky and Dioxazine Purple. Position the brush so that the paint-loaded side of the brush is lined up with the petal edge, and shade the tips of the upper two petals and the two side petals. With the same mixture, sideload the brush again and shade inside the throat of the violet. If necessary, wipe the brush and blend the paint.

4 Add Tints to Leaves, Deepen Shading on Daisy Centers and Highlight Flower Petals

Add interest to the painting by tinting some of the leaves. Side-load a lightly moistened no. 10 or 12 flat brush with Burnt Sienna. Position the paint-loaded side of the brush next to the leaf edge, and stroke this additional color onto the leaves. Notice that the leaf on the left has a brownish tint only on the tip, while the center leaf has the brownish tint on a much larger area. Don't be afraid to experiment; you may want tints on other leaves. Remember, it's your painting—please yourself. An optional tint mixture is Burnt Sienna plus a tiny amount of Dioxazine Purple.

Sideload a moistened no. 6 flat brush with Burnt Sienna darkened with a small amount of Burnt Umber and deepen the shading in the daisy centers.

To highlight the daisy petals, darken some Wicker White with a small amount of Linen. Thin this mixture with Blending Gel Medium and a small amount of water—the paint should be somewhat transparent for this step. Using the no. 4 filbert brush, stroke the back and side petals from the tips toward the center. Stroke the front petals from the center outward. Remember that you can sparingly moisten the surface with Blending Gel Medium and a bit of water to aid in blending and to keep the paint soft in appearance.

Highlight the upper violet petals where they fold out from the throat. Lightly moisten a no. 4 or 6 flat brush and sideload with a mixture of Wicker White and a small amount of Purple Lilac. Position the brush so that the side with paint is lined up with the fold of the petal, and stroke across each upper petal. Wipe the brush and blend if necessary.

5 Create Further Definition Within the Painting

To achieve dimension, additional shading must be applied to the leaves underneath the flower petals. Darken some Wintergreen with a tiny amount of Burnt Umber and Night Sky. Sideload a lightly moistened no. 10 or 12 flat brush with this mixture. With the paint-loaded side of the brush next to the daisy petals, stroke this deep color across the leaf. Wipe the brush and blend the paint if necessary. Deepen the shading on any leaves that appear to be underneath others, using the same brush and shading mixture.

Thin the shading mixture used on the leaves with water and, with a 10/0 liner brush, paint the veins in the leaves. Take care that the vein lines are not too dark or prominent.

Separate the daisy petals by painting the dark triangles you see where the petals attach to the daisy centers. Use the 10/0 liner brush and the dark shading mixture used on the leaves.

Thin a mixture of equal amounts of Dioxazine Purple and Night Sky with water and use the 10/0 liner brush to paint veins in the violet petals. Stroke the veins from the outer tips inward on the two upright and two side petals, as well as on the bud at the lower left of the design. Stroke the veins on the lower large petals from the throat outward.

6 Add Highlights

The leaves require no additional brushed-on highlighting since they were painted to allow the basecoat to show through, creating highlights.

I use two different brushes to stroke the highlights on the daisy petals. First use the no. 4 filbert to stroke the highlights on the back and side petals. These highlights should be a bit subdued, so add a tiny bit of Linen to Wicker White. Thin the paint with Blending Gel Medium and stroke the highlights from the tips of the petals toward the center of the flower. Take care that the paint is not too opaque and bright. Second, use a no. 2 round brush and Wicker White with the tiniest amount of Blending Gel Medium to highlight the front petals. Flatten the brush slightly as you load it, then stroke the highlights from the center of the flower outward toward the tips of the petals. The highlights on the front petals should be brighter and more opaque than those on the back petals.

Highlight the violets using the no. 2 round brush and a mixture of Wicker White and a tiny speck of Dioxazine Purple. Stroke the highlights on the two upper petals where they fold out from the throat. Stroke the highlights on the side petals from a point near the throat of the flower outward toward the tips of the petals. Brush highlights on the lower petal from the tip toward the throat. It takes very little paint and very few strokes to adequately highlight these small flowers.

Tip

I sometimes find that it helps to sparingly moisten the surface with Blending Gel Medium that has a tiny amount of water mixed with it prior to stroking on highlights. This is especially true for the petals that I want to have a softer, more subdued highlight. ❧

7 Begin to Finalize the Painting

Use the 10/0 liner brush to paint stamens in the center of the daisies. Mix Wintergreen and tiny amounts of Dioxazine Purple and Burnt Umber to achieve this rich color, then add enough water to the paint mixture so that it has the consistency of ink.

Using the tip of the 10/0 liner brush, add tiny dots of pollen on the two side petals of the violets. Be careful that these accents are not too prominent.

Again, using the 10/0 liner, paint the stems of the background foliage. Use Raw Sienna plus a small amount of Burnt Umber, thinned with water to the consistency of ink, for the golden-hued foliage. Use thinned Bluebonnet for the blue foliage.

Using the 10/0 liner brush, accent the tips of the violet calyx on the bud in the lower left of the design with thin strokes of Wintergreen.

8 Continue Adding Final Touches

Use the tips of the bristles on the 10/0 liner brush to add tiny dots of Sunflower over the daisy stamens to represent the pollen. Take care not to add too many, since additional lighter dots will be painted later.

If necessary, stroke additional highlights of Wicker White plus a speck of Dioxazine Purple on the two upright petals where they fold from the throat. Use the 10/0 liner brush and tiny amounts of paint.

Now paint the golden-hued background foliage. I used a no. 6 flat brush, which results in a leaf with a somewhat squared tip. A no. 4 filbert brush will also work nicely, giving a more rounded leaf. Use a mixture of Raw Sienna that has been darkened with a tiny amount of Burnt Umber and thinned with water. Paint these small leaves, using a slightly curved stroke, from the tips of the leaves toward the stems. Paint several leaves with one brushload of paint. The leaves should be transparent and remain in the background, enhancing the design, not competing for attention.

9 Complete the Detail

Paint a soft background around the design. This is simple to accomplish if you apply paint in a small area, then blend before moving to adjoining areas. Do not apply background color to the entire design at once—you will risk the paint drying before all the paint is blended to your satisfaction. I generally apply paint in about a two-inch square (5.1cm × 5.1cm) area, wipe the brush and blend before continuing. If I see that the premoistened surface is drying, I just brush a bit more of the Blending Gel Medium on to ensure a moist surface on which to work.

First, moisten the entire surface with Blending Gel Medium mixed with a small amount of water. Using the 1-inch (2.5cm) flat brush, brush this mixture well beyond where you expect to have any background. Now sideload the no. 12 flat brush with Bluebonnet mixed with just a speck of Wintergreen and apply the paint along the edge of the foreground design. Wipe the remaining paint from the brush and blend with short, overlapping strokes pulled in different directions. Be sure that the paint fades away at the outer edges so there is no harsh definition between the painted background and the applied background. Occasionally, load the brush with a hint of Dioxazine Purple to add a tint of this color into the background.

Use the no. 6 flat or no. 4 filbert brush and very thin Bluebonnet to paint the blue background foliage, keeping the paint very transparent with Blending Gel Medium and a bit of water.

With the tip of the 10/0 liner brush, add a few dots of Lemonade to the daisy stamen.

Tip When blending, you will probably brush some of the background color onto a few flowers and leaves. You can easily remove any unwanted background color with a clean, damp brush. ❦

10 Complete Your Project

In keeping with the design and clean lines of the chest, I chose to add only simple, sponged panels accented with gold on each side. My panels are 2¼″ wide (5.7cm) with 1″ (2.5cm) borders all around. You can adjust the width or length of your panels somewhat if you are painting on a different surface, or using a different-sized chest.

First, use the clear ruler and a sharpened chalk (or soapstone) pencil to measure and mark the lines indicating the edges of each panel. Use masking tape to protect the border, and place the tape against the marked lines. Run your finger over the edge of the tape to make sure it is firmly adhered. Now use a small piece of slightly dampened natural sponge to lightly "print" very thin Bluebonnet onto this panel, beginning at the taped edges. Very little sponging, if any, will be necessary near the design since you have already painted a background there. Sponge the feet of the chest also.

Make a *very* thin mixture of Bluebonnet, Blending Gel Medium and water. Use the 1-inch (2.5cm) flat brush to stroke this color on the rounded edges of the bottom and lid.

You can use a hairdryer on low setting to speed the drying of the sponged panels. Before you remove the masking tape, use the ¼-inch (0.6cm) dagger brush to paint a line all around each panel with Pure Gold Metallic thinned with water to the consistency of light cream. Position the brush on the edge of the sponged panel using the masking tape as a guide. The raised edge of the tape will help keep the line straight and your stroke steady as you paint each line. Remove the tape once all lines are painted.

Brush undiluted Pure Gold Metallic onto the bottom edges of the feet. Two coats of paint will be necessary for a smooth,

opaque coverage. Allow the paint to dry between coats.

Thin more Bluebonnet with water. Load a large flat brush with very thin paint, hold the brush with one hand, then pull the index finger of your opposite hand over the bristles to create spatters over the entire chest. You can also spatter by holding the brush in one hand and lightly tapping it on the wrist of your opposite hand. The further away from the project you hold the brush, the larger an area you will spatter—I hold the brush approximately 6″ (15.2cm) from the surface when spattering. You might also try using an old toothbrush when you spatter. It's always a good idea to practice a bit before you spatter onto your painted piece.

Sponge and spatter the insides of the chest as you did the panels. After all paint is dry, varnish the piece inside and out. I like a brush-on, waterbase varnish, such as Plaid's Satin Finish. The varnish will make the colors in the painted design more vibrant, as well as protect the painted finish.

> *Tip*
>
> It takes very little paint-and-water mix in the natural sponge to achieve the subtle effect you see in the finished project. If you dab the sponge repeatedly in one area, the watery paint marks will bleed together. ❧

About the Artist

Ginger Edwards has been painting for almost thirty years. Her interest in drawing began as a child, and although she was encouraged by her parents and teachers, she did not become involved in painting until after her own children were born. "I became acquainted with a lady who was taking painting classes and was absolutely enthralled with her paintings," says Ginger. "She encouraged me to sign up for a class and, sure enough, I have never laid my brush aside. I have painted almost every day since my first class."

Ginger began teaching classes with a few ladies gathered around her kitchen table. Before long, she opened a small shop and continued teaching. From that modest beginning, she began travel-teaching and has now authored many instructional books and pattern packets. Ginger paints in acrylics, oils and watercolors. She feels blessed to have been able to earn a living doing something she also enjoys as a means of relaxation. ❦

Deanne Fortnam, MDA

PEACHES A-PLENTY

When I began painting in 1982 and first sideloaded a brush, I fell in love with acrylic paints. At that time I painted only folk art pieces, because everyone thought if you wanted to create sharp focus realism, you had to paint in oils.

As my tastes changed and I wanted to expand my painting horizons, I found I was very limited by the sideloading techniques I knew at that point—I could only create value changes against the edges of objects. As time went by and I began exploring the limits of working with floated color, I discovered that you could achieve value changes wherever you wished. By learning how to manipulate your brushes and controlling the amount of water on the brush and the surface, it is possible to paint as realistically as you wish with acrylics, without using any retarding medium.

Once I discovered how to work realistically with acrylics, I fell in love with them all over again. Now I love the challenge and fun of painting fruit. This peach design has a soft, blended, blue-green background that complements the red-orange colors in the peaches. If you review the step-by-step illustrations, you can see that this project is not as difficult to paint as the finished project appears. In fact, it's a lot of fun, and I hope you'll give it a try. ❦

Materials

- wooden tray available from Covered Bridge Crafts, 449 Amherst Street, Nashua, NH 03063; (603) 889-2179

- DecoArt Americana acrylic paints
  Antique White
  Asphaltum
  Black Green
  Colonial Green
  Cranberry Wine
  Deep Midnight Blue
  Green Mist
  Hauser Dark Green
  Hauser Medium Green
  Jade Green
  Light Buttermilk
  Light Avocado
  Moon Yellow
  Napa Red
  Neutral Grey
  Olde Gold
  Taffy Cream
  True Ochre
  Yellow Ochre

- Winsor & Newton brushes
  series 995, 1-inch (2.5cm) and ¾-inch (1.9cm) flats
  series 500 nos. 8, 10, 12 and 14 flats
  series 530 no. 00 script liner
  series 520 no. 1 round

- Loew-Cornell brushes
  series 7200 no. 10/0 fan brush
  series 7600 ¾-inch (1.9cm) filbert mop
  series 7500 nos. 8 and 10 filberts

- Bette Byrd series 410 ⅜-inch (1cm) deerfoot

- palette knife

- Masterson Sta-Wet Palette

- waxed strip palette

- your usual acrylic painting supplies

1 Prepare Your Project

Seal and sand both sides of the tray with an acrylic-compatible sealer. Use a tack cloth to clean off all the sanding dust. Basecoat the flat inside of the tray with Jade Green. Basecoat the background again with thinned Jade Green. While this is still wet, pick up Hauser Dark Green on a ¾-inch (1.9cm) filbert mop and blend this from the lower left to the upper right using "slip-slap" motions of the brush. Repeat this a couple of times, always starting in the lower left corner. When you have sufficiently darkened the lower left side, pick up Light Buttermilk and blend this from the upper right of the tray toward the lower left, again using "slip-slap" motions of the brush. You are looking for a gradual change of value from light to dark, leaving some brush marks showing. Let this dry, then transfer the pattern lightly.

Palette Set-Up

Because I usually work with some color mixes, it is necessary to keep the paint workable until the project is finished. I use a Masterson Sta-Wet Palette without the palette film or sponge that comes with it. Instead, I dampen some good quality paper towels and lay a couple of layers in the bottom of the palette. When I set up my colors, I put them in order from lightest to darkest values and place the paints directly on the dampened paper towels. As you are working, mist the palette frequently with clean water and cover the palette whenever you take a break or are finished painting. If you set up your palette in this manner, your paints will remain workable until you finish your project.

Set up your palette using the value scales on the next page. That way, when the instructions call for the dark orange value, you simply go to the orange values on your palette and pick up the darkest one, rather than worrying about actual color names.

Loading the Brush

The real trick in achieving a realistic look is controlling your sideloaded brush. It is important to have the correct amount of water in the brush. If the paint corner of the brush is dragging and skipping, there is not enough water in the brush. Just lightly touch the loaded corner of the brush into some clean water, then blend the brush again on your waxed palette and it should work more smoothly.

The more common problem is having too much water in the brush. If you consistently leave a "halo" of color on what should be the clean water corner of the brush, or if the paint doesn't seem to stay where you want it to stay and keeps bleeding away, you are probably working with too much water. To fix this, lightly blot the water corner of the brush on clean paper towels, then blend the brush again on a clean spot on your waxed palette. If the paint has traveled to the water corner of the brush, it is usually best to rinse and start the sideload over again.

Don't short-change the amount of time it takes to properly load and blend the brush on your waxed palette. With floated color in acrylics we do our blending on the palette and no amount of fussing with your surface will fix a bad load. Be patient, learn to correctly sideload a brush and all your painting will become less effort and more fun!

Painting Procedure

To paint this design, it's best to start with the shadow leaves that fall under the right-hand peaches, then paint the two upper leaves that are behind the peaches. Next, paint the peaches, and last the branch and leaves that fall on top of the left-hand peach. The branch and leaves on the right side of the design can be painted at any time.

Shadow Leaves

Make a wash of the Medium Cool Green mix plus some water, and paint the shadow leaves indicated by the dashed lines on the pattern (see page 56). Mix a small amount of the Dark Cool Green mix into the Medium Cool Green mix and use this to sideload some shadows on the left sides of the leaves and on one side of the center veins. On the two center shadow leaves only, highlight opposite the shadows on the center veins and the right sides of the leaves with "washy" sideloads of Green Mist.

Color Palette

Antique White   Light Buttermilk

Warm Greens

Very Light Warm Green =
Jade Green

Light Warm Green =
1 part Light Avocado +
1 part Jade Green

Medium Warm Green =
3 parts Hauser Green Medium +
1 part Neutral Grey

Dark Warm Green =
2 parts Hauser Green Medium +
1 part Black Green

Very Dark Warm Green =
1 part Hauser Green Medium +
2 parts Black Green

Hauser Dark Green

Cool Greens

Very Light Cool Green =
2 parts Antique White +
1 part Green Mist

Light Cool Green = Green Mist

Medium Cool Green =
3 parts Hauser Green Medium +
1 part Colonial Green

Dark Cool Green =
3 parts Hauser Green Medium +
1 part Deep Midnight Blue

Very Dark Cool Green =
2 parts Hauser Green Medium +
1 part Deep Midnight Blue +
1 part Black Green

Asphaltum

Yellows

Very Light Yellow = Taffy Cream   Light Yellow = Moon Yellow   Medium Yellow = Yellow Ochre   Olde Gold   True Ochre

Oranges

Light Orange =
5 parts True Ochre +
1 part Napa Red +
a trace of Yellow Ochre

Medium Orange =
3 parts True Ochre +
1 part Napa Red

Dark Orange =
Cranberry Wine +
a trace of Yellow Ochre

W = Warm Greens
C = Cool Greens

2 Basecoat the Peaches and Begin the Highlights

Basecoat the peaches with a smooth, opaque application of Yellow Ochre (the medium yellow on your palette setup), ignoring the clefts, which we'll paint later when we shade the fruit. Begin highlighting the peaches with large "bull's eyes" of Moon Yellow (the light yellow on your palette) in the upper right of the three peaches at the top of the design. A "bull's eye" is a soft, circular highlight away from an edge. To create this, first sideload the brush with the appropriate color, then lightly and evenly dampen the surface of the painting with clean water. (It's very important that this not be too wet. If it is, the paint will keep bleeding away from where you place it and will be very difficult to control.) Place the loaded corner of the brush in the center of the highlight area and walk the brush around this center point, always keeping the loaded corner facing the center of the highlight area. There will be no highlights on the bottom peach. The light value you see is the basecoat color. I used a ¾-inch (1.9cm) filbert mop to create these large, Moon Yellow "bull's eyes," but you can use a 1-inch (2.5cm) or ¾-inch (1.9cm) flat brush if you wish. Reinforce the first highlight with a second sideload of Moon Yellow, walking the color out so that it covers two-thirds of the fruit.

3 Reinforce the Highlights

Reinforce the highlights with sideloads of Taffy Cream (the very lightest yellow on your palette), applying this color in a smaller area than the first highlights. Anytime you go lighter in value, make sure to keep it in a smaller area so the next highlight doesn't completely cover the previous value. I still used a ¾-inch (1.9cm) filbert mop to place this second highlight, but I used less pressure on the brush and didn't walk the paint out so this lighter value would cover a smaller area.

This is as light as the highlights will get on these peaches. They won't have a high shine of white because peaches are fuzzy and don't bounce back as much light as hard, shiny fruit like apples do.

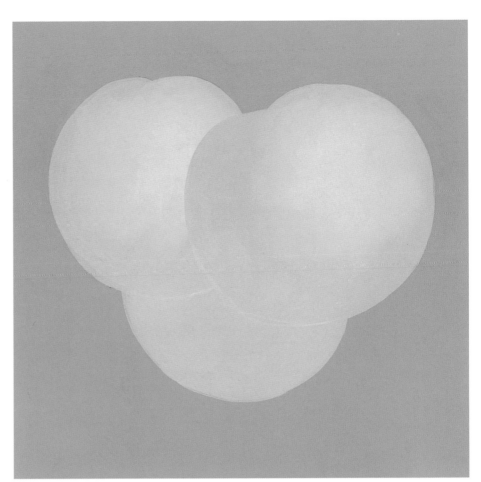

4 Begin the Shading

Begin the shading with large sideloads of the Light Orange mix on a 1-inch (2.5cm) flat brush, beginning on the lower left of the peaches. Make sure to walk this color out two-thirds of the way into the fruit. The first shadow and the first highlight will overlap. Reinforce this value a second time. Then, using a smaller flat (I used a no. 12) sideloaded with the Light Orange mix, shade around the rest of the peaches, as well as against both sides of the clefts.

5 Reinforce the Shading

Reinforce the shading on the lower left sides of the peaches with the Medium Orange mix using a ¾-inch (1.9cm) flat. Remember, the darker the value, the smaller the area it will cover. Also, bring a small amount of this value into the clefts and around the tops of the peaches and into the cast shadow areas, using a smaller brush than you used for the first shading. Be sure to keep the upper right sides of the fruit much lighter in value than the lower left sides. Darken the shadows on the lower left and the cast shadow areas with sideloads of the Dark Orange mix.

6 Detail the Peaches

Sideload "washy" floats of True Ochre on the two upper right peaches. To create the lovely, realistic-looking streaking on the fruit, first dampen the peaches with clean water and then drag streaks of the Dark Orange mix from the stem ends outward, following the growth direction of the fruit. I painted this with a sideloaded filbert. If necessary, soften with a clean damp filbert. You can reinforce the streaking as much as you feel necessary. Some peaches are quite strongly marked, so it would not be wrong to add even more color than you see in this sample. You can paint some streaks using straight Cranberry Wine in the darker value areas of the peaches.

Lightly stipple with Yellow Ochre (the medium yellow) over the peaches. Next, lightly stipple the peaches with the Light Orange mix and then last with Cranberry Wine in the shaded areas. Very lightly stipple with Taffy Cream (the lightest yellow on your palette) in the highlight areas on the three upper peaches.

Brush mix a small amount of the Light Orange mix into Yellow Ochre on a 10/0 fan brush and paint the fuzz on the outside edges of the peaches. This fuzz *must* be very, very short and fine.

7 Basecoat Leaves and Branches and Begin Leaf Highlights

Referring back to the pattern on page 56, basecoat the leaves marked "W" with the Medium Warm Green mix and the leaves marked "C" with the Medium Cool Green mix. I will discuss painting the "W" leaves only, but both the warm and cool leaves are painted in the same manner; just use the cool green value scale (shown on page 55) to paint the cool green "C" leaves.

Begin highlighting the warm green leaves with sideloads of the Light Warm Green mix. Where the sideloads are not against the edges of the leaves, lightly dampen the area to be highlighted with clean water, then sideload a no. 8 or no. 10 filbert. Keeping the loaded edge facing the center of the highlight area, create the oval-shaped highlights.

To create the V-shaped highlights where the leaves are ruffled, lightly dampen the area with clean water, then side-load a no. 10 flat with the Light Warm Green mix. Start with the chisel edge of the brush against the outside edge of the leaf, with the loaded edge facing the middle of the highlight. Leading with the water corner of the brush, bring the brush up and around, ending with the chisel edge of the brush against the outside edge. Remember to keep the loaded corner of the brush facing the center of the highlight area.

Basecoat the branch with Asphaltum.

8 Reinforce Leaf Highlights and Begin Highlighting Branches

Reinforce the highlights on the warm green leaves with sideloads of Jade Green (the lightest warm green on your palette), then in the lightest value areas with Antique White. Anytime you are building values either lighter or darker, make sure to "stack" the values. The lighter or darker the value gets, the smaller the area it covers. Decreasing the size of the brush used as you lighten or darken the values will make it easier to control the size of the highlight or shadow.

Mix some Antique White into Asphaltum with a small round brush. Flatten the brush so that it forms a chisel edge. With the chisel edge of the brush, highlight the tops of the branches using choppy motions with the brush.

9 Shade Leaves and Reinforce Branch Highlights

Begin to shade the warm green leaves with sideloads of the Dark Warm Green mix against both sides of the center veins using a no. 10 or no. 12 flat. To paint this "back-to-back" sideload, lightly dampen the leaf with clean water, shade one side of the center vein, then flip the brush over and shade the other side of the center vein, softening where the loaded edges meet. This avoids the buildup of a hard line in the center of the shaded area. Shade the rest of the dark areas with sideloads of the Dark Warm Green mix, then reinforce the shading in the darkest value areas with sideloads of the Very Dark Warm Green mix. Remember to stack your values.

Make a very light mix of Antique White plus a small amount of Asphaltum and use this to reinforce the highlights on the tops of the branches. Use a small round brush flattened into a chisel edge, using choppy motions with the brush as you did for the first highlights in step eight.

10 Finish the Leaves and Branches

Paint a few warm accents on the leaves with washy sideloads of Olde Gold. The red accents are "washy" sideloads of the Dark Orange mix or the Medium Orange mix. Keep these very subtle.

Pull the vein lines with a script liner and thinned Medium Warm Green mix. Shade under the side veins with a no. 8 flat side-loaded with the Dark Warm Green mix. Shade against one side of the center veins with the Very Dark Warm Green mix. Remember that the cool green leaves will be painted in exactly the same manner as the warm green leaves, but using the cool green value scale.

Brush mix Black Green plus some Asphaltum with a small round brush and shade the bottoms of the branches with short, choppy strokes of the flattened chisel edge.

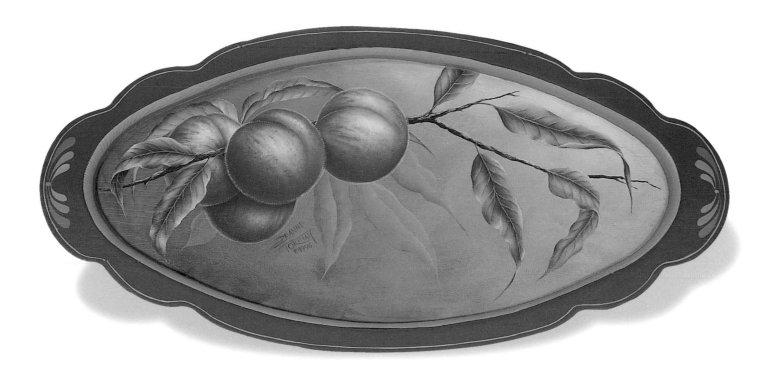

11 *Finish Your Project*
Basecoat the inside and outside edges of the tray with Green Mist (the next-to-lightest cool green). Basecoat the top of the flange and the back of the tray with a mixture of 10 parts Hauser Dark Green + 1 part Jade Green. Paint a stripe ³⁄₁₆″ (.5cm) from the outside edge with Green Mist. Paint the outside sets of comma strokes with the dark green basecoat plus a small amount of Green Mist, so they are slightly lighter in value than the background. Lighten this with a little more Green Mist and paint the next sets of strokes. Lighten again with more Green Mist and paint the inner strokes and a small oval between the strokes.

Varnish the tray with an acrylic-compatible spray, or brush on a varnish of your choice.

About the Artist

Deanne Fortnam began decorative painting in 1982. (The first time she sideloaded a brush, it was love at first sight!) She joined the Society of Decorative Painters in 1983 and was awarded its prestigious Master Decorative Artist certification in 1991. A popular seminar instructor, Deanne teaches throughout the U.S., and internationally. She lives in her hometown of Nashua, New Hampshire. ❦

Priscilla Hauser, MDA

TIME TO PAINT ROSES

Don't you think it's time you learned to paint roses? To me, they're the most beautiful flower, and roses carry more special messages than any other flower I paint.

Painting lovely roses requires several skills: lovely brushstrokes, proper double loading of the brush (getting the brush full of paint), understanding proper paint consistency and, last but not least, *practice.* I tell my students to paint no less than one hundred roses, step-by-step, carefully placing and executing each stroke as they go. By the time you too have completed the hundredth rose, you will be very proud of your effort and will paint lovely roses forevermore. ❦

Materials

- *miniature wooden clock by Walnut Hollow, available at most craft and hobby stores or through mail-order suppliers*
- *FolkArt Artists' Pigments (these are high-quality acrylics like those found in tubes, packaged in squeeze bottles for your convenience)*
  Titanium White
  True Burgundy
  Hauser Green Dark
  Hauser Green Medium
  Hauser Green Light
  Green Umber
  Ice Blue
  Pure Black
  Pure Gold
- *Loew-Cornell brushes*
  series 7300 nos. 6 and 8 flats
  series 7350 no. 1 liner or scroll
- *Masterson Sta-Wet Palette*
- *palette knife*
- *Plaid FolkArt Blending Gel Medium or Extender*
- *brush basin*

- *paper towels*
- *sandpaper*
- *tack cloth*
- *brown paper bag (unprinted)*
- *sponge brush*
- *Scotch brand Magic Tape*
- *ruler*
- *eraser*
- *tracing paper*
- *white chalk*
- *pencil or stylus*

- *waterbase varnish*
- *optional oil supplies*
  If you would prefer to paint this design in oils, substitute oil paints in the same colors for the acrylics, Priscilla's Choice red sable brushes (Loew-Cornell series 9030) in the same sizes as the acrylic brushes and use a tracing paper palette pad instead of the Masterson Sta-Wet palette.

1 *Prepare Your Project*

Sand the clock, if needed, and wipe with a tack cloth. Using the sponge brush, basecoat the clock with Pure Black. When dry, apply a second coat. When the second coat is dry, rub the surface with a piece of unprinted brown paper bag to smooth the grain. To create the trim, use Scotch brand Magic Tape to mask off a band approximately ½″ (1.3cm) wide, securing the edges of the tape to the clock by rubbing them down with an eraser. Apply two or more coats of Pure Gold to the trim area. When dry, use a good liner brush full of thinned Hauser Green Medium to carefully stripe the outside edges of the gold band. A second coat may be needed to cover thoroughly. Neatly trace the pattern onto a sheet of tracing paper. To transfer the pattern, I prefer to use white chalk—that way you don't have to worry about trying to remove pattern lines or lines showing through the paint. Use the chalk to retrace the pattern lines on the back of the traced design, then shake off excess dust. Center the design on the surface and carefully retrace the lines with a pencil or stylus. Don't press too hard or you will make an indentation in the wood.

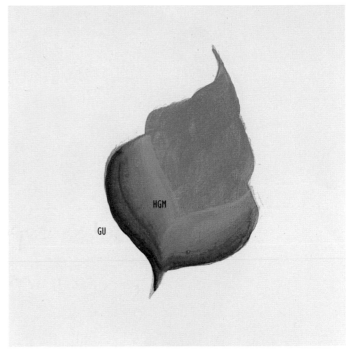

2 Basecoat the Leaves

Many people are afraid to paint leaves, but all they require is time to practice the technique so the strokes flow beautifully from the brush onto the surface you're painting. The leaf technique I'm presenting here is a variation of my basic-brush-stroke, dry-brush blended leaf, done in acrylics. Fill your flat brush good and full of paint and basecoat the leaf with Hauser Green Medium. Apply a neat, smooth second coat to cover thoroughly. Let dry. (To paint this leaf in oils, simply omit the basecoat.)

3 Apply Medium and Anchor Shadow

Apply Blending Gel Medium or Extender. Double load the brush with Hauser Green Medium and Green Umber. Blend on the palette to soften the colors in the brush, making sure your brush is good and full of paint. Pat on the shadow color at the bottom of the leaf. If desired, you can let this color dry to "anchor" the shadow—this way the Green Umber won't slip when you blend.

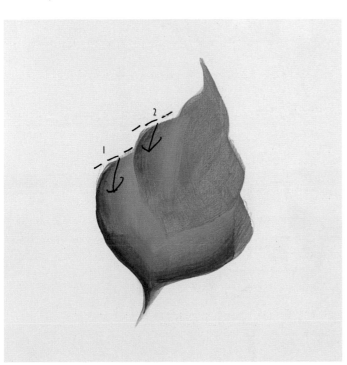

4 Paint Shading Strokes One and Two

If you allowed the color to dry in the last step, apply fresh Blending Gel to the leaf. Double load your flat brush with Hauser Green Medium and Green Umber. Blend on the palette to soften the colors in the brush, making sure the brush is good and full of paint. Reapply the shadow at the bottom of the leaf (this moist application will be blended later, while the underneath "anchored" shadow will not be disturbed). Place a second stroke above the first, as shown.

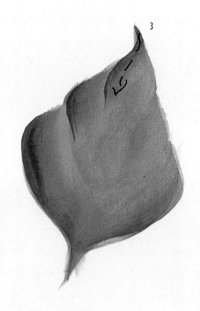

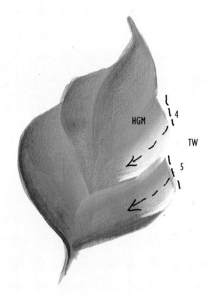

5 Paint Shading Stroke Three
The center stroke is an incomplete S-stroke, which forms the top of the leaf. To paint this stroke, stand your brush on the flat edge with the dark side pointing up. Pull slightly and let the brush roll to the left, applying pressure on the brush.

6 Add Highlight Strokes
Double load your brush with Hauser Green Medium and Titanium White. Blend on the palette to soften the color. Paint two comma-like strokes on the right side of the leaf, opposite the shading strokes. Angle these strokes outward, with the brush pointing inward toward your nose.

7 Add Additional Lights
Wipe your brush and add a small amount of Hauser Green Light and a touch of Titanium White to the center of the leaf.

8 Merge the Colors
Wipe the brush again and gently merge the leaf colors together. Add a touch of True Burgundy to the shadow area, if desired.

9 *Blend*
Wipe your brush and start blending at the base of the leaf. Using a light touch, pull toward the first stroke. Next, pull toward the second stroke, then up toward the center, then toward the fourth and fifth strokes. This is called directional blending.

10 *Blend in the Reverse Direction*
Now pull from the outside edges very lightly back toward the base of the leaf. Don't overblend or muddy the leaves. Work quickly, as the acrylic paint dries very quickly.

11 *Finish the Leaf*
Apply a vein of Green Umber and Hauser Green Medium. You can accent the edges of the medium value leaf with a little Ice Blue, if desired. Change the value of the leaf by using Hauser Green Dark or Hauser Green Light in place of the Hauser Green Medium in the previous steps.

Color Palette

   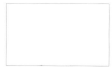

True Burgundy   Dark value   Medium value   Light value

You may make as many values of these beautiful burgundy colors as desired. Start by adding a good deal of True Burgundy to Titanium White to mix the dark value color. Next, take some of the mixed color and add a lot of Titanium White to mix a medium value. Last, use a lot of Titanium White, with just a tiny touch of the medium value mixture, to create an icy pink color for the lightest value. You may paint roses in several values or all in the same value. The following demonstration is for a medium value rose. To paint a dark value rose, use the dark value mixture and True Burgundy. To paint a light value rose, use the light value mixture and the dark value mixture.

Light value rose

Dark value rose

Medium value rose

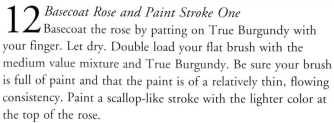

12 Basecoat Rose and Paint Stroke One

Basecoat the rose by patting on True Burgundy with your finger. Let dry. Double load your flat brush with the medium value mixture and True Burgundy. Be sure your brush is full of paint and that the paint is of a relatively thin, flowing consistency. Paint a scallop-like stroke with the lighter color at the top of the rose.

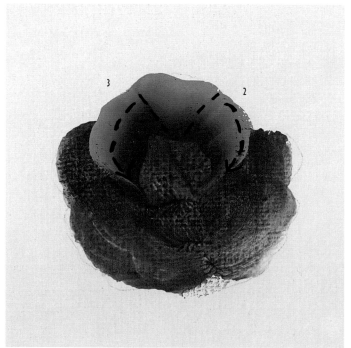

13 Paint Strokes Two and Three

Paint a scallop-like comma stroke on the right side of the first stroke. Paint a scallop-like comma stroke to the left of the center.

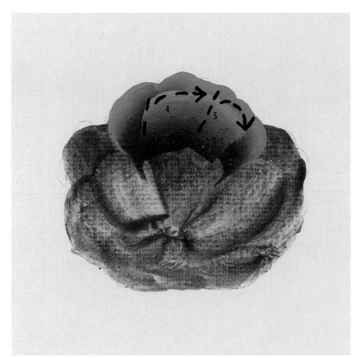

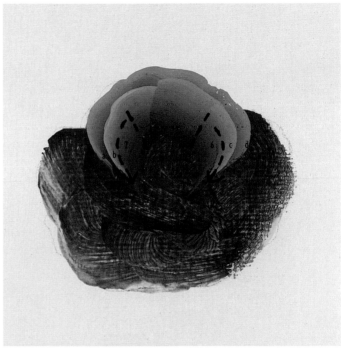

14 *Paint Strokes Four and Five*
Pick up more paint for the second row of petals. Paint these scallop-like strokes staggered in between the first row of petals you painted—you don't want the strokes to line up.

15 *Paint Strokes Six and Seven*
Paint two more comma-like strokes, completing the second row of petals. You should now see four "tails" or edges of the strokes, labeled "a" through "d."

16 *Form the Base of the Rose Bowl*
Double load the brush with paint and stand the brush on its flat edge. Connect the tail of the comma stroke marked "b" to the tail marked "c." You will paint a U-stroke as you connect the two tails.

17 *Paint the Petals Around the Bowl of Rose*

The outside edge of the rose is composed of five strokes. Four are scalloped comma strokes. The center stroke is more of an S-stroke.

18 Paint a Second Bowl
Another bowl is now painted on top of the first one, this time connecting tail "a" to tail "d." This will be another U-stroke.

19 Add Fill-in Petals
The fill-in petals are perhaps the hardest of all to paint. They are painted on top of the outside petals you painted previously.

20 *Paint a Rolled Front Petal*
It is lovely to roll a petal over the front of the rose. It looks like the petal is cupping up over the center of the flower. This is called a "rolled S-Stroke." The stroke connects the tail of one fill-in petal to the tail of another.

21 *Finish the Rose*
Finish the rose by carefully filling in the center with True Burgundy. Then paint scallop-like strokes in an upward manner to form the final inner petals. With the desire and willingness to practice, you *will* paint these roses.

22 *Seal the Project*
When you are done painting the design, let the piece dry and cure, then apply two or more coats of waterbase varnish.

About the Artist

Priscilla Hauser MDA, founder of the National Society of Tole and Decorative Painters, is an internationally known artist and teacher. She has introduced decorative painting to tens of thousands of students worldwide through her workshops, books, videos and series of instructional television programs. Her first book, *For Whom the Brush Toles*, has sold over a million copies. Her latest book, *Priscilla Hauser's Book of Decorative Painting*, was published by North Light Books in 1997. Her work appears regularly in magazines such as *Decorative Artist's Workbook*.

Today, students come by the hundreds to Priscilla's Studio by the Sea on the Florida panhandle. Here, Priscilla joyfully teaches brushstrokes and beautiful blending to beginning and experienced painters alike. 🖌

Louise Jackson, MDA

BLUE IRIS

*S*omeone started a rumor years ago that watercolor is the most difficult medium to use. But we all know that each medium demands skills that may take practice to learn. If you are proficient in another medium and just approaching watercolor, allow yourself to be a beginner again. All that you know from your use of other mediums will come into play as soon as you master some control of the water.

The secret to the watercolor technique I used to create *Blue Iris* is to paint on very wet paper for as long as possible. I was able to get as far as shown in step one before I stopped to dry the paper. If you cannot get that far because the paper feels so dry that the color pulls and causes brush marks, simply dry the paper completely. Then wet it again and proceed from where you left off. Basically, this is a two-stage painting. Just remember to keep painting on wet paper until the first stage is complete. ❧

Materials

- *11" × 15" (29.9cm × 38.1cm) sheet of Winsor & Newton rough watercolor paper*

- *Winsor & Newton watercolors*
  Cobalt Blue
  Indanthrene Blue
  Indigo
  New Gamboge
  Permanent Rose
  Winsor Orange
  Winsor Violet

- *Brushes*
  no. 20 synthetic flat
  1-inch (2.5cm) natural hair flat
  no. 10 round sable

- *tracing paper*

- *wax-free graphite paper*

- *two water containers (one for rinsing your brush and one for clean water)*

- *palette (I use a Zoltan Szabo covered palette)*

This pattern may be hand-traced or photocopied for personal use only.
Enlarge at 143% to return to full size.

Color Palette

New Gamboge

Winsor Orange

Permanent Rose

Cobalt Blue

Indanthrene Blue

Indigo

Winsor Violet

Mixes

Indigo + New Gamboge

Permanent Rose + Cobalt Blue

Cobalt Blue + Permanent Rose

Terms and Techniques

Here are a few watercolor terms and techniques to help you get started:

Dry—Dry the paper until it is bone dry. You will not feel any dampness or coolness to it at all. This means it is dry inside as well as on the surface.

Layering—To work with a layering method, the most important thing is to dry the paper thoroughly before applying the next layer. If the paper is not completely dry, the water inside may mix with the new water and create blooms or lines that you hadn't planned on.

Lift out color—Apply a damp brush to the area where you wish to remove color. Allow the water to loosen the pigment, then lift the pigment with a thirsty (dry) brush.

Scrub the edges to soften—Dampen a worn-down, soft, synthetic brush or a scrubber and straddle the hard line that you are trying to soften. Gently scrub up and down along the line, moving a little pigment into the white area and creating another value change.

Wash—A wash is a thin layer of paint, applied as evenly as possible. Always work into the wet edge of the paint. ❧

1 Apply Washes to Very Wet Paper

Trace the drawing onto the watercolor paper using wax-free graphite paper. Wet the paper so that the water sinks in. Apply water several times so it will sink in evenly.

Using the 1-inch (2.5cm) flat brush, start with the colors on the upper left part of the paper. Apply New Gamboge near the closed bud, then some Cobalt Blue and Indanthrene Blue to the outside. You will be painting the dark background colors later.

When the paper has lost its shine, alternately apply Indanthrene Blue and Winsor Violet to the iris's lower petals (called the "falls") and the lower bud. Apply these colors so they are slightly *above* the edge of the petal drawing. This will create a white edge. Pull the colors from the outside inward, toward the stem. If you find that you have painted this too solidly, you may lift out light areas with a damp brush.

Paint in the rest of the background, being careful to leave a white edge on the iris. Paint the background with thicker mixes of Indigo, Indanthrene Blue and Winsor Violet.

Paint a green color on a couple of the leaves and on the bud leaves by using a mix of Indigo and New Gamboge. Use a damp no. 20 flat brush to chisel out some lighter lines on the leaves. Then soften these colors so they fade into the background. This entire step should be done on damp paper.

2 Dry the Paper and Rewet the Details

This illustration shows only the areas you'll be painting in this step. Because you'll want to rewet the top petals of the iris with water, this is where you should stop to dry the paper first. Then rewet one of the upper petals (called "standards"). Using a warm pink mix of Permanent Rose with a little Cobalt Blue, apply the color and soften the edges with a thirsty brush. Dry this petal and paint the next one in the same manner.

Use Cobalt Blue and a little Winsor Violet for a cool mix and apply this as the shading on the ruffles and dips and rolls. Each time you paint a petal, dry it before painting the one next to it.

Shade inside the iris with a thin wash of Indanthrene Blue. Use a little darker mix on the innermost tiny petals.

Now let's paint the closed bud: Use Indigo and New Gamboge mixed to a green to paint the bud foliage. Keep the center of the bud light to create a rounded form. Paint the bud petals with Winsor Violet and Indanthrene Blue mixed together. Apply the color along one side on dry paper. Use the no. 20 flat

brush with half of the water removed to blend the transition line. Allow this half to dry, then repeat on the other half.

To add form and depth to the larger, partially opened bud, lift out the light areas with a damp brush. You may use a little Indigo to create a small, dark delineation between the front and back petals.

Paint tiny lines at the top of the fuzzy beard with Winsor Orange. Paint a few more tiny lines with New Gamboge.

To complete the iris, paint the underside of the petal on the far right with a mix of Indanthrene Blue and Winsor Violet. Paint the darkest area near the stem. Pull the color outward to create a lighter value at the edge of the petal.

The darkest darks of the background occur underneath the iris. Paint Indigo between the left petal and the lower bud and fade it out. Using a mix of Indigo and New Gamboge, paint in the green stem showing through from the upper bud. Paint in a few negative shapes around the leaves and stem at the bottom using Indigo.

3 Check Your Work

Soften any edges that appear hard with clean water, especially the ruffles and folds, being careful to maintain the white edge of the petals. If necessary, deepen the strongest darks of the forward petal's ruffles with Winsor Violet, but don't overwork it. The beauty of transparent watercolor is that it allows the white of the paper to shine through, giving vibrancy and life to your beautiful blue iris.

About the Artist

Louise Jackson has authored thirteen books on how to paint in oil, acrylic and watercolor. The most recent is titled *Painting Flowers in Watercolor With Louise Jackson* (published by North Light Books in 1997). Louise teaches nationally as well as internationally and has hosted a TV series on decorative painting. In 1991, she achieved the honor of being named a Master Decorative Artist. Her paintings appear in several museum and corporate collections.

Louise lives in Dayton, Ohio with her husband Ken. They have four children and four grandchildren. 🍎

Sherry C. Nelson, MDA

HOUSE SPARROW AND HOLLYHOCKS

House sparrows aren't true sparrows but come from a family called "weavers." They were introduced from Europe in the late 1800s. Abundant and aggressive, they have become a common sight in the cities and countryside of North America. I chose the old door as the setting for this painting to emphasize the close relationship between this species and the humans with whom they share their habitat. ❧

Materials

- wooden tray available from Cabin Crafters, P.O. Box 270, Nevada, IA 50201; (800)669-3920; or use 14" × 11" (35.6cm × 27.9cm) piece of ⅛"-thick Masonite panel

- Delta Ceramcoat acrylic paint in Red Iron Oxide

- Accent acrylic paint in Wicker

- Winsor & Newton Artists' oil paints
  Burnt Sienna
  Burnt Umber
  Cadmium Lemon
  Ivory Black
  Permanent Magenta
  Raw Sienna
  Raw Umber
  Sap Green
  Titanium White
  Yellow Ochre

- Winsor & Newton brushes series 710 nos. 2, 4, 6.and 8 red sable brights
  series 7 no. 1 red sable round

- a synthetic flat brush

- odorless thinner

- cobalt drier (optional)

- palette knife

- paper towels

- disposable palette for oils

- dark graphite paper

- tracing paper

- gold leaf

- gold leaf adhesive sizing

- ballpoint pen

- sponge roller

- cotton cheesecloth

- tack cloth

- old toothbrush or spattering tool

- wood sealer

- newspaper for work surface

- 220-grit wet/dry sandpaper

- Krylon Matte Finish #1311

- Krylon Spray Varnish #7002

- Krylon Crystal Clear Acrylic Coating #1303

Color Palette

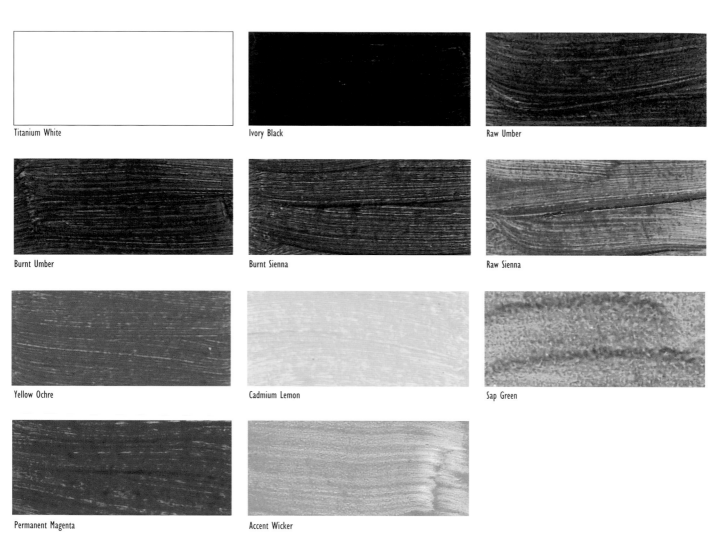

Titanium White

Ivory Black

Raw Umber

Burnt Umber

Burnt Sienna

Raw Sienna

Yellow Ochre

Cadmium Lemon

Sap Green

Permanent Magenta

Accent Wicker

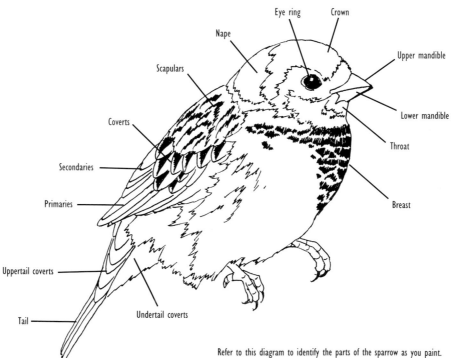

Eye ring

Crown

Nape

Upper mandible

Scapulars

Lower mandible

Coverts

Throat

Secondaries

Breast

Primaries

Uppertail coverts

Tail

Undertail coverts

Refer to this diagram to identify the parts of the sparrow as you paint.

This pattern may be hand-traced or photocopied for personal use only. Enlarge at 145% to return to full size.

1 Prepare the Surface

Begin by sealing the front, back and sides of the wooden tray with wood sealer. When the sealer is dry, sand lightly with the wood grain using 220-grit wet/dry sandpaper. Wipe the tray with a tack cloth to remove sanding dust.

Paint the tray bottom (or Masonite panel) with Accent Wicker acrylic paint. Let dry and recoat. Let dry again, then spray with Krylon Matte Finish #1311.

Paint the shaped edge of the tray with Delta Ceramcoat Red Iron Oxide and spray with Krylon Crystal Clear Acrylic Coating #1303 to make a smooth base for the gold leaf. Apply gold leaf sizing to the Red Iron Oxide areas with a synthetic flat brush. Let the sizing dry until it turns clear. Cut a pad of gold leaf to a strip just a little larger than the width of the area to be leafed. Holding the leafing by the tissue interleaves, apply pieces of gold leaf to the edge of the tray, always overlapping the previous leaf. When all areas to be leafed are covered, use a soft pad of cotton cheesecloth to press the leaf firmly onto the surface. Let dry several hours. Brush off excess leafing with cheesecloth, then spray with Krylon Crystal Clear once again.

When the gold leafing is complete, the entire tray can then be stained, including the gold leaf. Squeeze out a 2″ (5cm) stripe of Raw Umber oil paint onto a palette. Add a drop of cobalt drier with the tip of a palette knife. Then add several scoops of odorless thinner with the palette knife and mix until the paint is evenly thinned. The consistency should not be so thick as to hold a peak (like whipping cream) and not so thin that it runs off the palette. When the proper consistency is obtained, use a synthetic flat brush to apply stains in the corners of the tray, edges of the routing and any other areas that are hard to reach. Then wipe on additional stain in the corners of the tray using cheesecloth. It's okay if some stain gets on the painted tray bottom.

With a clean piece of cheesecloth, wipe off the excess stain, pulling and blending the stain with the direction of the wood grain. Buff the surface until it is evenly covered. Soften any stain on the painted tray bottom, buffing it into the painted surface. Rub the gold leafed areas softly to remove most of the stain. When you're pleased with the overall effect, allow the stain to dry. Spray the tray bottom with Krylon Matte Finish Spray #1311 and the remainder of tray with Krylon Spray Varnish #7002 (gold leaf should never be sprayed with a matte finish—it dulls the glow).

Transfer the pattern on page 87 to the prepared surface, using dark graphite paper. Be especially careful when transferring the detailed wing feathers and the eye and beak areas. Also, go ahead and transfer all the breast spots. You'll work around them while basecoating and will have them for a guide when placing the markings. For best results, make the transfer as accurate as possible.

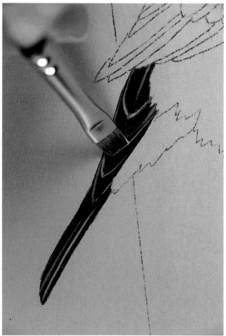

2 Basecoat the Tail

Basecoat the tail and upper tail covert area with a firm application of straight Raw Umber, using a no. 4 bright. Do not rinse your brush (see sidebar on next page). Draw feather lines into the wet paint with a stylus.

3 Separate the Feathers

Sparsely load the dirty brush with white paint. Create feather lines with the chisel edge of your brush, beginning at the tip of the feather and working toward the base. If you can see both sides of the feather, do each side separately, beginning at the tip. Messy feather lines can be cleaned up with Raw Umber.

Background Option

If you don't wish to paint your sparrow on a tray, you can use a Masonite panel. Prepare as for the tray bottom, except the Masonite panel does not need to be sealed before painting. ❦

4 *Basecoat the Wing*
Basecoat the primary wing feathers with a mixture of Burnt Sienna + Raw Sienna. This transparent mix should allow graphite lines to show through, eliminating the need to use the stylus. Under each feather line, lay a narrow shadow area of Raw Umber + Ivory Black. Blend a little to soften the bottom edge of color into each feather. This helps the feathers to look overlapped.

5 *Basecoat the Covert Area*
Now basecoat the covert area with the same mix, again retaining graphite lines for reference. Shade the left half of each feather in the top row with an area of Ivory Black + Raw Umber. Add a bit of shading to separate the other short covert feathers below this row.

6 *Add Feather Lines*
Again load the dirty brush in sparse white, picking up a dry gray mix to use for all the feather lines. Do the longer primary feather lines with a no. 6 bright and the shorter feather lines of the coverts with a no. 4 bright. Remember, if you can see both sides of the feather, it must be done in two steps, with the lines meeting at the tip of the feather. Add a few shaft lines with the same dirty white.

Dirty Brush

It's so unusual for me to wash the paint out of a brush while working that when it is necessary, the instructions in the project will say so; otherwise, use a dirty brush. Washing a brush takes out all the little bits of dirty color, which is what helps you tone and control the intensities in your painting. If you used clean color on the brush at every step, you would have a much more difficult time keeping those strong colors subdued. For the most part, keep the lid on the thinner and keep your flat brushes out of it. We'll use thinner to make the paint more workable for some detailing, usually with the round brushes. ❧

7 *Basecoat the Scapular Area*
Use a mix of Burnt Sienna + Raw Sienna to basecoat the scapular area above the coverts. Lay color on next to and between the markings so you can still see them. Block in a dark shadow form of Ivory Black + Raw Umber next to the wing.

8 *Detail the Scapular Area*
Thin Ivory Black + Raw Umber with odorless thinner. Add the scapular detailing with this mixture on the no. 1 round brush. Vary the lengths and sizes of the markings.

9 *Basecoat the Undertail Coverts and Breast*
Basecoat the undertail coverts and breast with a light value, a warm gray mixture of Titanium White + Ivory Black + Raw Umber. Using the no. 6 bright, basecoat with choppy strokes, following the growth direction of the bird as color is laid on. Fluff some of the choppy strokes over the edge of the dark shadow next to the wing.

10 *Detail the Breast*
Apply shadow areas with a little Raw Umber and a little Ivory Black, loaded together on a dirty brush. Lay the paint onto the surface with a bit of pressure in each area of shadow. Wipe the brush, then chop the edges of the darks to connect them to the light basecoat. Let brush tracks show for texture and interest. Now thin a mix of Ivory Black and Raw Umber and, using the round brush, detail the markings on the breast. Use the line drawing on page 86 as a guide for size and placement. Add highlights with clean white on a clean no. 6 bright. Pressure on areas of white, then chop them into the surface for texture as you did for the shading color. See step eleven for instructions on creating depth.

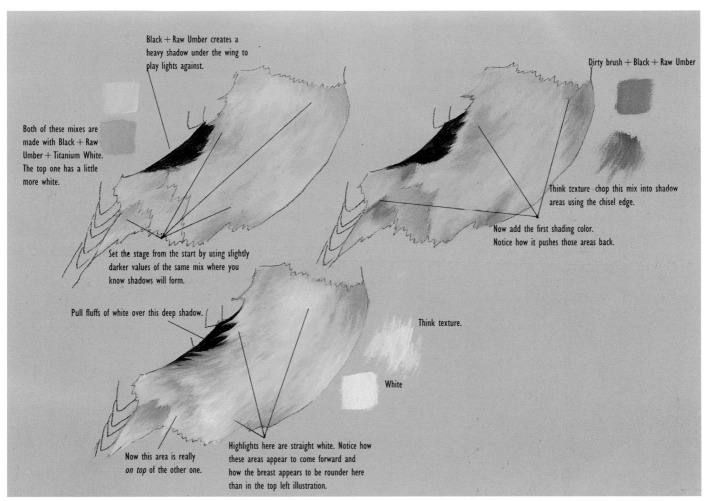

Black + Raw Umber creates a heavy shadow under the wing to play lights against.

Both of these mixes are made with Black + Raw Umber + Titanium White. The top one has a little more white.

Set the stage from the start by using slightly darker values of the same mix where you know shadows will form.

Pull fluffs of white over this deep shadow.

Now this area is really *on top* of the other one.

Highlights here are straight white. Notice how these areas appear to come forward and how the breast appears to be rounder here than in the top left illustration.

Dirty brush + Black + Raw Umber

Think texture chop this mix into shadow areas using the chisel edge.

Now add the first shading color. Notice how it pushes those areas back.

Think texture.

White

11 Create Depth by Playing Light Against Dark

This illustration shows you how to create depth in the sparrow's breast. Remember, darks recede and lights come forward. A gradation of value from light to dark creates shape and form.

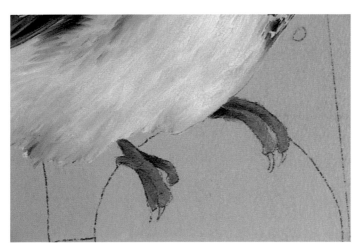

12 Basecoat the Feet

Basecoat the feet with Raw Sienna. Shade a bit where the feet go under the feathers and between the toes with Raw Umber. The no. 2 bright works well for this small area.

13 Detail the Feet

Add a line of dirty white (the white picked up on a dirty brush) down the center of the toes and leg. Wipe the brush and blend the line a little to soften it into the basecoat. Add detail segment lines across the legs and toes. Toenails may be added now, using thinned black and the round brush, or you can wait until you've finished painting the doorknob.

14 *Basecoat the Eye*
Basecoat the eye ring with Raw Umber + Titanium White, using the point of the round brush. Wash out the round brush in thinner and blot dry. Pick up Ivory Black to fill in the eye. Add a dot of white for the highlight in the eye. Now basecoat around the eye area with a mixture of Ivory Black and Raw Umber, using a no. 4 bright. Narrow down the eye ring carefully, leaving just a faint, light line in front of the eye. Leave the eye ring wider behind the eye.

15 *Fill in the Beak*
Using the no. 2 bright, fill in the top half of the upper mandible of the beak with Raw Umber. Using the chisel edge, add a line of Raw Umber where the mandibles meet. Also use Raw Umber to add a teeny bit of shading on the bottom of the beak. Now fill in the rest of the beak with Yellow Ochre + Cadmium Lemon.

16 *Detail the Beak*
Wipe the no. 2 bright and blend between the umber and the yellows on the upper mandible. Create a smooth value gradation by blending on the line where the colors meet. Next, dab on a little white with the point of the round brush. Put more white on the lower mandible than on the upper. Now wipe the round brush and flatten the tip of the bristles to make a little blender brush. Tap into the white highlight you applied and stipple the color into the surrounding areas. Lift the brush off the surface with each tap.

17 *Basecoat the Rest of the Head*

Now fill in the rest of the head area with the following colors: For the crown, use Ivory Black + Raw Umber + Titanium White; for the nape, Raw Umber; and for the rust area between crown and nape, use Burnt Sienna. Fill in light areas of the throat with Titanium White, the dark patch to the left of the throat with Raw Umber, and finish with a little area of black below the beak. Notice that as I applied the colors, I laid them on carefully, following the zigzags and notches of the pattern lines; however, I did not blend or connect any areas together.

18 *Begin Blending the Head*

Now, with a dry no. 4 bright, begin blending *just* where the colors meet, following the growth direction of the bird's feathers. Move the chisel edge back and forth across the line where two color sections come together. Lots of short strokes kept very close together will create the feathery texture that you're looking for. Add a bit of shading at the top of the crown with Ivory Black + Raw Umber. Soften the edges of this color into the basecoat also.

19 *Highlight the Crown*

Add a white highlight on the crown. Soften it into the surrounding basecoat. Add just a bit of chopped-in dirty white on the Burnt Sienna patch and soften with just a little blending.

20 *Fill In the Doorknob*
With a sparsely loaded no. 6 bright, begin laying in dark shadow color on the doorknob with Ivory Black + Raw Umber. Apply color with random strokes of the brush, crisscrossing each one to form a patchy look. Wipe the brush, then load a bit of white on it to make a midvalue gray. Use this to fill in the remaining area, again sparsely.

21 *Begin Blending the Doorknob and Add Rust*
Begin blending, just on the line where the colors meet. Use the same brush action for the blending as you did for applying the color. Don't set the brush down and pull it—that will overblend the colors and make them muddy. Wipe the brush dry and load with a little bit of Burnt Sienna. Lay a few strokes of this in the *middle* value areas to give a suggestion of rust. If you have lost the darks, you can reinforce them with the addition of black in the darkest shadow area. Highlight with dirty white just a bit where the light hits most strongly.

22 *Begin Filling In the Doorplate*
Begin laying in the darkest areas of the doorplate using a no. 6 bright. Each time you load the brush, pick up a different one of these mixes so the browns are varied: Ivory Black + Raw Umber, Ivory Black + Burnt Umber, straight Burnt Umber, and straight Raw Umber. Fill in the keyhole with black. Note how the edges of the dark color applications are rough, sparse and uneven. That will help them blend readily.

23 *Fill In the Rest of the Doorplate*
Fill in the remainder of the doorplate with dry Burnt Sienna, blending and softening it into the dark values to create good gradations. With the chisel edge, lay a fine line of Raw Umber + Titanium White on the left edge of the keyhole.

24 *Detail the Doorplate*
Add circular brads in the corners of the doorplate with black and highlight them with a line of white. Now begin patting and softening on some very muted highlights, using Raw Sienna plus dirty white on a bright brush. Soften the highlights into the basecoat a bit. Now use the same mix on the round brush, detailing some of the highlight areas to appear rough and pitted.

25 *Create Wood Grain*
Using thinned Raw Umber on the no. 8 bright, wash on streaks and lines resembling wood grain. Place this thinned color on the entire door area, but do a section at a time so that color can be wiped down before it dries.

26 *Soften the Grain*
Using a piece of cheesecloth, rub and soften the thin Raw Umber streaks into the background. This step is easier to do when the bird is dry, of course. When you've finished wiping one section, apply thinned paint to another in the same manner and rub that down.

27 *Spatter the Door*
When all Raw Umber streaking is complete, you can spatter the surface to obtain the effect of age and old paint. Thin Raw Umber with odorless thinner in a puddle on your palette. Using an old toothbrush (not the one you use every day!), dip a few bristles on the end into the mix. Then, using your palette knife to scrape across the bristles, spatter the mix onto the surface. The thinner the mix, the lighter and larger the spatters will be. A thicker mix produces a fine fly-specking. I use some of each mix to produce a varied look. Don't worry about getting a little paint on the bird or other areas. It will blend easily into a wet bird and wipe off a dry one. Practice this technique on newspaper before applying it to your surface.

28 *Paint the Door Frame*
Treat the frame areas of the door much the same as you did the background of the door. Use a wash of Raw Sienna applied with the large bright. Lay color on with the direction and patterning of wood grain. I used more Raw Sienna than I did Raw Umber and covered the frame areas more heavily. I then wiped them down with cheesecloth to soften the effect. If you wish to spatter these areas, too, complete all the areas before beginning to spatter with the Raw Umber.

29 *Basecoat the Dark Area Behind Bird*
Basecoat the dark area of wood behind the bird with black, then Raw Umber, alternating these colors as you apply them with the large bright. Blend the darks together when you've finished basecoating this strip. It should be very dark with just a little wood grain showing. You can see I've continued with the thinned Raw Umber areas to the left of the dark area. Lay on the thinned paint, and then wipe down and spatter, if desired.

30 *Basecoat the Hollyhocks and Leaves*
The dark value on the hollyhocks is a mix of Permanent Magenta and a tad of Raw Sienna. Fill in with the no. 6 bright, base-coating with the growth direction. Wash the brush, blot dry and load with Raw Sienna + Titanium White. Use this mix to basecoat the remaining flower petals. Notice how I merged the color mixes in a zigzag, but did not blend them. The dark area on the leaves is blocked in with Ivory Black-+ Sap Green. The light leaf value is made by wiping the dark value from the brush and loading into a white "loading zone" pulled from the Titanium White. This mix should be a light greenish value. Meet the colors in a choppy, broken line.

31 *Blend and Highlight the Hollyhocks and Leaves*
Blend the hollyhock colors with the chisel edge of the brush, just where they meet. Don't let the magenta travel out too far into the light value. Then begin high-lighting, using white applied with pressure in areas of strongest light; however, do not outline the petal with white. With a dry brush, blend the highlights softly into the petal. Blend the leaves with the chisel edge of the brush from the edge of the leaf toward the center, leaving little or no space between the strokes. Leaf high-lights may be added with a lighter value of the greenish leaf mix and blended in the same manner.

32 *Finish the Painting*
Continue blending highlights on the petals until they are softened. If more white is desired, re-highlight a few areas for emphasis. Add the central vein structure on the leaves with the light value leaf green mix. Basecoat the round yellow flower center with a mix of Yellow Ochre + Cadmium Lemon. Then dab on a little gloppy white and stipple it around to create a textured white highlight. Apply yellow lines around the center with Cadmium Lemon and a tiny bit of Permanent Magenta (to make a darker yellow) on the round brush. You may thin this mixture if it doesn't move easily.

Finishing
When the sparrow painting is complete and has dried thor-oughly, spray it with Krylon Spray Varnish #7002. Attach the handles to the tray and drop in the glass or Plexiglas tray bottom, cut to size, to cover and protect the painting.

About the Artist

Sherry C. Nelson is internationally known for her paintings of realistic birds, wildlife and florals, and she teaches her techniques with skill and authority. Seminars taught in forty-eight states and several foreign countries have given her the opportunity to share both her love of birds and animals and her special and unique techniques for painting them. Sherry's skill in breaking the painting process into easy-to-understand steps has given even the entry-level painter an opportunity to excel using her methods.

Sherry has been an active member of the National Society of Decorative Painters since its founding. The Society recognized her exceptional painting skills with the Master Decorative Artist certification. She is a past President of the organization and received the prestigious Silver Palette Award in recognition of her promotion of decorative painting worldwide.

Sherry has authored eighteen instructional publications for the decorative artist and has done numerous videos, packets and other materials, which are available for the student of birds, wildlife and florals. Her book, *Painting Garden Birds With Sherry C. Nelson, MDA*, was published by North Light Books in the spring of 1998. If you would like additional information, as well as her current seminar schedule, please write to Sherry in care of The Magic Brush, Inc., P.O. Box 16530, Portal, AZ 85632. ❦

Jackie O'Keefe

MICHELLE'S ROSE

Around the turn of the nineteenth century—in what we loosely call the Victorian era—a new method of printing in color, called lithography, was developed. This new way of printing allowed excellent reproductions of flowers, children, birds, butterflies—or any other wonderful whimsy created by artists—to be printed in vivid color, at a fraction of the previous cost. The reduced cost of lithography made it possible for small businesses and industry to use color printing in their advertising and promotions. Business cards were no longer limited to simple black-on-white printing, but included colorful roses and birds on black or white paper. The consumers of the Victorian era were so entranced with this inexpensive artwork that it became a pastime for ladies and young children to collect the reproductions, cut out the fanciful designs and paste them into scrapbooks, a practice that has been revived in this turn of the century.

This design is done in a style I call "Victorian floral." Painted on a black background, the single rosebud is stylized into a round, plump shape, the highlights and darks are overemphasized and the lilies of the valley and bleeding hearts are simplified. Then the whole composition is romanticized with a name or sentiment on a flowing banner or ribbon. I designed this project for students who asked for a class to improve their skills in sideloading acrylic paints to float color on a simple design. Although the design has a lot of parts to it, none of them is complicated, and there is no light source to create difficult cast shadows.

Feel free to change the name to suit your purposes, or even use a short phrase like "Love Is Patient" to personalize the banner. I've included a copy of an alphabet for you to trace—enlarge or reduce your word or phrase to fit the space. Also consider enlarging or reducing the design if you wish to paint it on some other surface. You can substitute yellow roses for the pink ones by using three values of yellow to replace the pinks. The banner could become a ribbon by changing it to a pastel color and creating a picot edge with tiny dots or by making higher shines in the highlight areas to make it look like satin. Make this project your own! ❧

Materials

- wooden box, available from Allen's Woodcrafts, 3020 Dogwood Lane, Route 3, Sapulpa, OK 74066; (918) 224-8796

- DecoArt Americana acrylic paints
  Burnt Umber (DA064)
  Lamp (Ebony) Black (DA067)
  Antique White (DA058)
  Antique Green (DA147)
  Mink Tan (DA092)
  Light Cinnamon (DA114)
  Raw Umber (DA130)
  Mocha (DA060)
  Buttermilk (DA003)
  Shading Flesh (DA137)
  Crimson Tide (DA021)
  Avocado (DA052)

- Winsor & Newton Regency Gold Brushes
  series 560 ¼-inch (.6 cm) and ⅜-inch (1cm) angle shader
  series 540 no. 0 short liner
  series 550 nos. 2 and 4 filberts

- 180-grit or higher sandpaper

- no. 000 black wet/dry sandpaper

- tracing paper

- fine-point black permanent pen

- J.W. etc. First Step Wood Sealer (or any other commercial sealer and wood stain)

- J.W. etc. Right Step Matte Acrylic Varnish

- white and gray graphite paper

- soft white eraser

- stylus

- mending tape

- water basin with ridges in the bottom

- Masterson Sta-Wet Palette (I use the 9" × 12" [22.9cm × 30.5 cm] version)

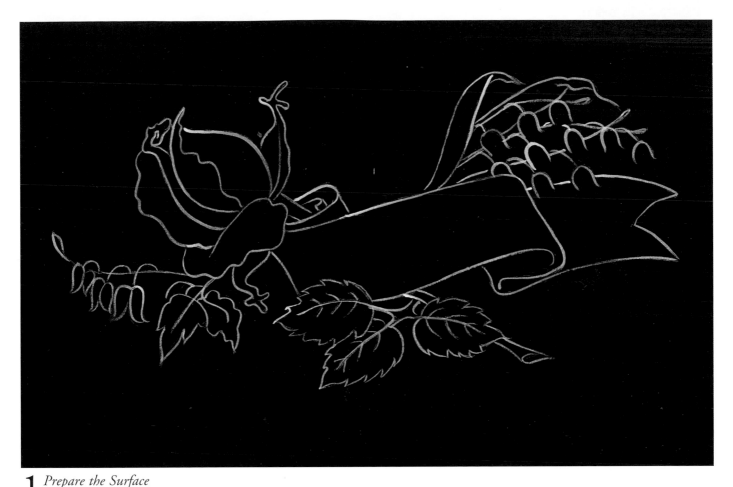

1 Prepare the Surface

Remove the lid from the box by pulling the pins out of the sides. Check for any rough spots and sand lightly with fine sandpaper, 180-grit or higher. Wipe with a damp rag to remove any sawdust or dirty residue. Stain and seal the wood in one step with a mix of 5 parts J.W. etc. First Step Sealer to 2 parts Burnt Umber. This should give you a transparent dark oak color. Don't go over any surface more than once, or the stain will become too dark and the contrast between the stained surface and painted area will not be noticeable. Be sure to cover all of the inside and outside surfaces. Allow to dry thoroughly. Trace the design onto tracing paper with a fine-point black pen,

copying only the lines you will need to help you with basecoating and shading. Center the design on the outside upper surface of the lid and tape one side down with mending tape. Slip a piece of gray graphite under the tracing and transfer the shape of the black area to the lid. Basecoat the rectangular shape with Lamp (Ebony) Black.

When the black paint has dried and cured, again position the traced design over the black rectangle and tape down one side with mending tape. Slip a piece of white graphite under the tracing and transfer the design to the surface with a fine-point stylus.

Start With a Wet Palette

It's important to use a wet palette, not just to keep your paints moist and workable, but also to sideload your floated color. Most of the work for sideloaded color is done on the palette. If you poke the point of your angle brush into a pile of paint and then pat-pat the brush on the wet palette, you can see the paint move toward the center of the brush. When you use a dry palette or paper to pat the brush, you will usually be out of paint before you achieve the smooth transition of color that you need for successful floated color. Dampen the surface of the painting site with clean water on a clean brush, then be sure to check your sideloaded brush before beginning to paint. If it has too much water on the clean side, pinch the excess water out of the brush, pushing the remaining water back toward the loaded side. The color should fade near the center of the sideloaded brush. If this is not so, clean the brush and start again. ❧

2 Basecoat the Design

Before you begin painting, be sure to read through all of the instructions, and check to see that the pattern has been transferred accurately. I like to apply all of the basecoat colors to all of the parts of the design, working the whole project at one time. This allows me to balance the highlights and shadows and build a focal area more quickly.

Dampen the bud of the rose and basecoat it with a medium wash of Mocha on the no. 4 filbert brush. One coat of paint will not cover the area completely because of the black background. Basecoat the banner with a heavy wash of Antique White on a dampened surface. Basecoat the stems, leaves and calyx of the rose with a medium wash of Antique Green. Note that I have left little black lines of the background color showing between the sections of the rosebud and the banner. This allows you to see where the graphite lines were.

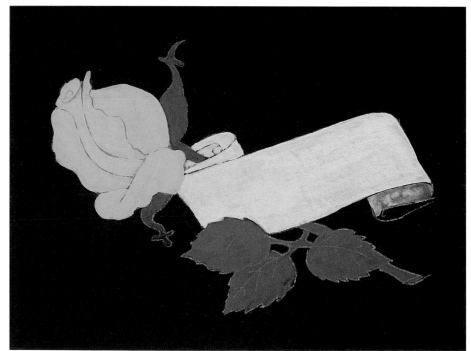

3 Add Second Basecoat

Over the previous basecoats, apply a second coat of Mocha on the rosebud, Antique White on the banner and Antique Green on the foliage. Notice that the fine black lines were covered with this coat of color, but they are still clearly visible for guidance. You can also see the white graphite through the Antique Green.

Dampening the Surface

Dampening the area to be painted before each step, even basecoating, will help avoid paint ridges and will give a smoother coverage. The paint can also be easily removed if you're not satisfied with the result, especially while sideloading. Just dampen with clear water on a clean brush and wipe off the excess moisture with the heel or side of your hand until the surface is damp, but not wet.

If you dampen each section as you paint and add water to all of your basecoat colors to create different densities of washes, you will still be able to see the details of the traced design after the basecoats dry—this eliminates having to reapply the pattern over the dried basecoat colors.

Be sure to allow the paint to dry thoroughly before dampening again and adding more layers for depth, contour and contrast. If you aren't sure if a section is completely dry, touch it with your finger. If it feels cool to the touch, it is not completely dry. If you try to dampen a section before the paints have dried, you are likely to create a hole as the wet acrylic paint lifts from the surface. ❧

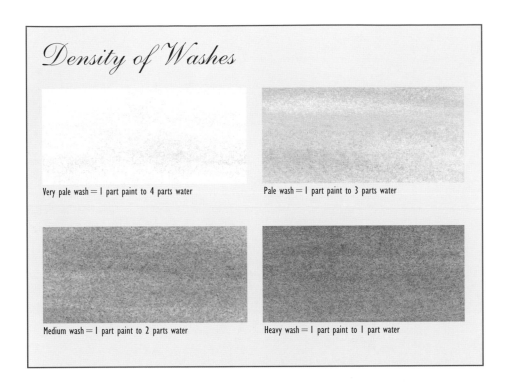

Density of Washes

Very pale wash = 1 part paint to 4 parts water

Pale wash = 1 part paint to 3 parts water

Medium wash = 1 part paint to 2 parts water

Heavy wash = 1 part paint to 1 part water

4 Finish the Basecoats

After the banner, rosebud and leaves have been basecoated, thin down the Buttermilk to a medium wash and, with the no. 2 filbert, fill in the lily of the valley flowers with two side-by-side comma strokes. This should be done with a one-coat coverage to maintain a look of transparency in the bells of the flowers. Stroke the bleeding hearts on the left side of the design with Shading Flesh on a no. 2 filbert brush. Paint the little pistils hanging down from their throats with the no. 0 short liner and a mix of Buttermilk + Avocado. The pistils should look like little tornadoes hanging between the comma strokes. Basecoat the leaves of the lily of the valley and bleeding hearts with medium washes of Avocado.

5 Add First Shading

The first shading color is the one that creates all of the shaping and contour of each part of the design. Each of the following steps may be repeated over and over again until the smooth transition of color and contouring satisfies you. Dampen the area before shading, work until it becomes tacky, then move to another while the first area dries. Then dampen the first area again and continue shading as needed. On a project this small, I suggest moving from the rose to the banner and back until you have completed the shading. As you connect one shadow area to another, remember that the bud is basically a spherical shape and the shadows should have curved edges.

The leaves, stem and calyx of the rose are shaded with Raw Umber on the ¼-inch (.6cm) angle brush. The leaves of the bleeding hearts and lily of the valley are shaded with a floated mix of 2 parts Avocado + 1 part Lamp (Ebony) Black on the ¼-inch (.6cm) angle brush. The flowers of the lily of the valley are shaded with the ¼-inch (.6cm) angle brush and a float of Antique Green down the right side of each flower. The bleeding heart flowers are shaded with a float of Crimson Tide spread horizontally across the top and bottom of the comma strokes.

Shading Triangular Shadow Areas

One of the reasons I use angle brushes is because I like to start shading in the little, tight triangular areas while I have the most paint on my brush. The tip of the angle brush fits perfectly into these triangular areas. Sideload your brush with the appropriate color and place the tip of the brush into the triangle, walking the color backward out of the area into the light. As you move backward out of the triangle, you will use up the paint and the color will become lighter. Do not walk forward or you will lose your sideload on the brush.

In the example on the left, I started in the tip of the triangle with a sideloaded brush but only pulled the brush up along the edges. This is incorrect: It does not create the illusion of shadow emerging into light but only outlines the two edges. In the right example, note that the color started in the tip of the triangle and was then pulled across the open space, connecting the two sides. As the paint fades so does the shadow. This is the correct way to create shadow and contour. ❧

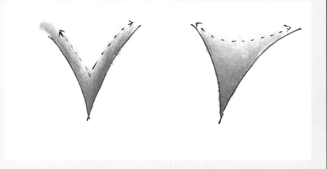

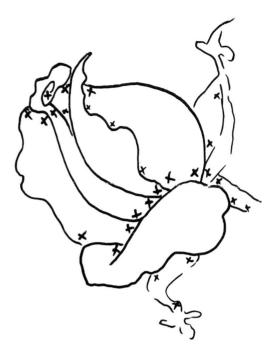

Shading Curving Edges

The rosebud is basically a spherical shape, so the shadows should have curved edges. To create the illusion that the sphere on the right is a round ball and not just a flat disk, it is necessary to make the disappearing edge of the shadow follow the curve of the ball. The dotted line represents the end of the shadows. This not only tells us that the right sphere is behind the left, but that the right sphere is round. ❧

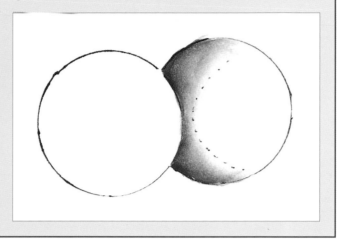

Shade the contours and petals of the rosebud with a sideload of Shading Flesh on the ¼-inch (.6cm) angle brush. In this drawing of the rosebud, notice the little "X"s in the points of the triangular areas. These are the tiny dark spots where most of the shadows will start. They are the areas where the least light can penetrate; start your shading here. If you learn to look for these triangles of dark, you will never have a problem with deciding where to start shading. As you move from one triangular area to another, you will find they will start to connect to each other.

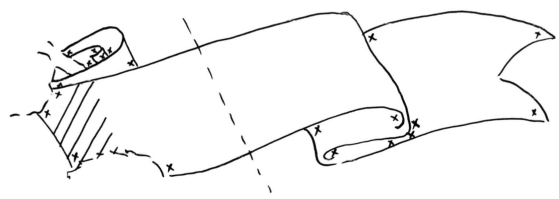

Many painters seem to have difficulty painting a curving banner or ribbon. They shade in all of the turns and folds as they should, but the object still appears to be flat and unbelievable. The key is to make sure your contouring shadows are long enough. Too often, when we start shading a banner or ribbon, we only shade along the edge and then wonder why it looks so flat. By moving the first shading color further out, you have created a wide enough area for later additions of darker values of color that will make the banner or ribbon appear more rounded and flowing.

The banner is shaded with the ⅜-inch (1.0cm) angle brush sideloaded with Mink Tan. To help you create a more realistic banner, I have placed a dotted line through the center of the top portion of the banner. Think of this line as the available area to paint. If you try to walk the shadow (represented by the diagonal lines) out one-fourth to one-third of the way toward the center, or highlight part of the banner, you will create a better illusion of shape. Each of the little "X"s represent little triangular areas where shadows start. Dampen each section of the banner and walk the Mink Tan out of the shadow into the light.

Lesson on Painting Round Leaves

I would like to share with you a mini-lesson in painting simple round leaves. ❦

1 Basecoat the leaves with a light wash of Antique Green.

2 With Raw Umber sideloaded on the ¼″ (0.6cm) angle brush, float little chunks of dark along each side of the center stem, leaving the area for the stem and side veins blank. On the upper leaf, the chunks of color fade about one-third of the way across the leaf. Place the ¼″ (0.6cm) angle brush with the sideload of Raw Umber against the outside edge of the wider part of the leaf and repeat the process along the outside edge, as a sort of continuation of the earlier shadows. This leaves a lighter highlight area between the two areas.

3 When the leaves are dry, float a sideload of Raw Umber under the edge of the upper leaf to create a cast shadow on the lower leaf. This establishes which leaf is on top or in front of the other.

4 The unshaded areas are the areas where highlights will probably be applied. Place a highlight of Buttermilk on the ¼″ (0.6cm) angle brush in a back-to-back sideload (pull a float of color along a line, then turn the project over and paint the other side of the line so the color fades away to each side of the line).

5 When the highlight is dry, wash a tint of Shading Flesh over the highlight area.

6 Add Additional Shadings

Often, a second or third shading color is needed to create even more shape and depth of color. These additional shadings will usually start in the smallest triangular areas and will always be spread over areas previously shaded with a lighter value of the color. Note that not all areas that were shaded before need additional color. This example has had additional darker shading added to the important parts of the project—the rosebud and the banner. It is not necessary to create strong contrasts and details in the background elements of the design because the rose and banner are the focal area. The smaller flowers and leaves are simply added interest and should be more subdued in color and contrast.

Look at the deepest areas of the dark on the rosebud. Place the tip of the ¼-inch (.6cm) angle brush sideloaded with a float of Crimson Tide at the tip of the triangles and walk the color out to cover about one-third of the previous shading. This adds a rich pink/red to the shadow part of the rose. The banner also has a second shading with a float of Light Cinnamon on the ⅜-inch (1.0cm) angle brush. Be sure to walk the color out to cover about one-third of the previous Mink Tan shading.

If desired, you can add a third shading color to the rosebud and banner. (The completed third shading is shown in the next step on page 108.) In the deepest recesses of the shadows on the rosebud, place a float of Crimson Tide + Raw Umber in the tip of the darkest triangles. This will only cover about one-third of the previous shading of Crimson Tide, so it is very tiny. On the banner, carefully place a float of Raw Umber in the folds and turns to simulate the darkest shadows.

7 Add the Highlights

Just as the shading becomes darker and darker as it fades from light, highlights need to be built up to a shine. As the highlight becomes brighter and lighter, it also becomes smaller. Note that the highlights on the banner are not as strong as the highlights on the petals of the rose. This is because we want the rose to be the first thing that strikes the eye. Then, as the eye moves, it will roll down to the banner and then on to the other less detailed elements of the design. The red areas on the diagram below show where the highlights should be placed on the design.

On the rosebud, first float a mix of Mocha + Buttermilk onto the fullest parts of each petal. On subsequent floats, add more and more Buttermilk to the mix, until you achieve the required shine. Also float a highlight of Antique Green + Antique White along the upper edge of the stem and at the cut on the bottom of the stem. Create the highlight on the banner with a float of Buttermilk. Use a back-to-back sideload on the flat parts of the banner and use the liner brush on the roll. Paint the highlights on the round rosebud leaves as explained earlier. Paint the highlights on the leaves for the bleeding hearts just as you did the rose leaves, using Avocado + Buttermilk. Create the shine on the flowers of the bleeding hearts with back-to-back floats of Buttermilk pulled horizontally across the fullest part of the flower. Highlight the flowers of the lily of the valley with a float of Buttermilk down the right side. With the liner brush, paint tiny comma strokes of Buttermilk across the mouth of each one. Highlight the leaves of the lily of the valley with a float of Avocado + Buttermilk along the right side of the forward leaf and also along the edge of the folds at the top of both leaves.

8 Add the Details

It's always attractive to add some tints of the other colors in the design to the flowers. If you wish to do so, you may use a float of Shading Flesh to add warmth to some of the lily of the valley flowers and tints of Shading Flesh to the leaves of the rosebud.

If desired, you can outline any elements that look a little fuzzy or undefined. Always use a very good liner brush (I used a no. 0 short liner) and the appropriate shading color to outline in a hit-or-miss manner (with broken pieces of lines). Continuous lines will make the element look stiff and awkward. By using the shading color, the lines will not be noticeable.

I outlined the rosebud here and there with Crimson Tide. Keep these lines very fine, not completely outlining but rather cleaning up fuzzy edges and creating divisions between sections. I outlined the banner with the second shading color, Light Cinnamon. I outlined the leaves of the lily of the valley and bleeding hearts with Avocado and painted in the stems with the same color. The stem and calyx of the rose can be outlined as needed with Antique Green.

Little details help to make the painting look more interesting.

Adding veins to the leaves, or little points to their tips, creates added dimension and pizzazz. The red lines on the banner help to draw the eye and create a frame for the later addition of personalization. Little touches of dark red in the deepest shadows on the rosebud add contour and contrast to the lightest highlights.

When you've painted all of the design, it's a good idea to put it aside for awhile and come back later to check for depth of contour and color. If you have a few days, put the project out of your sight. Little details will jump out at you when you have changed your focus for awhile.

This is a good time to check for graphite lines. Erase all those that you can with a soft white eraser. If they still show here and there, paint them out with the black background color. Clean up the areas around elements with black paint on a liner brush. It's hard to see float overruns on the black paint, and once you have applied the coat of varnish that will bring them out, it's too late. To see what the finished project will look like after it's been varnished, just wipe the whole area with clean water. All of the flaws and color mistakes will show up.

9 Paint the Scallop Design

Paint the scallop design around the outer edge of the black area with a liner brush and Lamp (Ebony) Black. First dot on Lamp (Ebony) Black dots with the handle of the liner brush. Space these evenly around the whole rectangle and allow to dry thoroughly. With the short liner brush and black paint, make scallop lines around each dot.

ABCDEFGHIJKLM
NOPQRSTUVWXYZ
abcdefghijklmn
opqrstuvwxyzr&

10 *Add Lettering*
The personalization on the banner is optional. If you wish to include lettering, you can simply use the sample alphabet above to trace the name or phrase of your choice. The easiest way to add lettering is to make a separate tracing of the center section of the banner. With a pen or pencil, make two dotted lines equidistant from the outside edge.

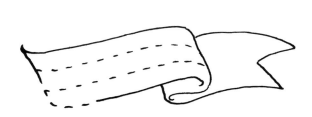

Lay this tracing over the alphabet and trace the desired name or word onto the paper. This will allow you to see if it fits the area properly. It may be necessary to enlarge or reduce the letters slightly to make them fit, or it may even be necessary to use a different font.

When you've worked out the details on the tracing paper and you are pleased with the results, transfer the name or phrase to the painted surface with gray graphite and a stylus. Check to be sure that the lettering is centered and follows the movement of the banner. Paint the lettering with black paint and a fine liner brush or, if you are uncomfortable with line work, try using a fine black permanent ink pen.

11 *Finish Your Project*
If you desire, you may antique the outside of the box with soft floats of Raw Umber. Dampen a side at a time and float a shade of color at the corners of the box and at the divisions of the wood. This should simulate darkening that has resulted from frequent handling.

I like to use a matte varnish for a finish on these boxes. It helps to enhance the illusion of age and doesn't refract light to draw the eye away from the painting. My personal preference is J.W. etc. Right Step Matte Acrylic Varnish. I use at least four coats, allowing the varnish to dry thoroughly between applications. If the surface becomes rough or bumpy from the acrylic varnish, a light sanding with no. 000 wet/dry black sand-

paper between coats is beneficial. Be sure to wipe the surface clean with a damp rag before applying another coat of varnish or the residue from the sandpaper will be trapped in the varnish. Varnish all surfaces, including the bottom and inside.

Replace the lid on the box by inserting the pins in the ends of the lid. You may also wish to line the inside bottom of the box. To enhance the illusion of age, stain old newsprint with tea or diluted brown paint and glue it to the inside of the box.

I hope you have enjoyed working on this Victorian floral design and that it has inspired you to look for other "Turn of the Century" art to enhance your decorative painting.

About the Artist

Jackie O'Keefe has been a member of the Society of Decorative Painters for over fifteen years and has taught at nine of the Society's national conventions. She has authored four *Personal Collection* books on decorative painting with Viking Folk Art Publications, and she recently published *Handlettering for Decorative Artists* with North Light Books. Her line of pattern packets sell around the world, and she has had articles on painting published in most of the current magazines for decorative painters.

Says Jackie, "As an artist, I can only give credit to God for the generosity of His gift to me. With each project I design and each lesson I write, I am working to enhance that gift and share it with others. As a woman, I give credit to my family and friends for their unfailing support and encouragement, especially to my husband, Pat." ❧

Jackie Shaw

FILETE AND FRUIT

Ethnic folk arts, crafts and music have always claimed a special place in my heart—none more so than filete (fee-lay-tay), the advertising art of the produce vendors of Buenos Aires, Argentina. I discovered it on my first teaching tour to Argentina, and it tugs at my heartstrings every time I return.

Filete, along with the tango, emerged in the late 1800s in the poorer section of Buenos Aires, among the greengrocers, brothels and shanties. Like the tango, filete was considered low class, offensive and vulgar. Also like the tango, it was full of swirls and rhythm (exactly the sort of thing I love to paint!). It was through my research on

this lively folk art that I developed a kinship with the people, the culture and that era of life in Buenos Aires.

While the tango went off to Paris to gain worldwide acclaim, filete rambled the streets of Buenos Aires, decorating horse-drawn grocer carts, wagons and (later) motorized trucks and buses. During the Perón dictatorship, filete was banned within city limits and quickly and quietly disappeared. It is now being revived among fine artists, graphic artists and decorative painters.

Like many folk arts, filete includes brush-stroke scrolls, fruit, vegetables, vignettes, angels, sayings—even dragons and animals. It is unique, however, in its

use of cast shadows and strong highlights, which seem appropriate for a stroke art that was to be seen outside, under the bright Argentincan skies.

Filete was painted with long-bristled brushes (some as long as three inches) that often did not have handles. Shadows and highlights were simply painted as bold strokes. Colors were vivid and bright. In this project, I have adapted the filete style for more subtle tastes with blended colors, and have used techniques and brushes you will find more familiar and easier to handle than their traditional counterparts. ❧

Materials

- 20" (50.8cm) diameter lazy Susan (or substitute round tray or table top) available from Weston Bowl Mill, P.O. Box 218, Weston, VT 05161; (802) 824-6219

- Grumbacher oil paint in Burnt Umber

- DecoArt Americana acrylic paints
  Antique Gold
  Antique Teal
  Black Plum
  Blue Haze
  Blush Flesh (optional)
  Cadmium Yellow
  Colonial Green
  Country Red

  Cranberry Wine
  Crimson Tide
  Dark Chocolate
  Deep Midnight Blue
  Hauser Light Green
  Hauser Medium Green
  Jade Green
  Light Avocado
  Milk Chocolate
  Mocha
  Olive Green
  Peaches 'n' Cream
  Pineapple
  Plantation Pine
  Raspberry
  Summer Lilac
  Toffee
  Yellow Ochre

- Loew-Cornell brushes
  series 7550 ½-inch (1.3cm)

  and ¾-inch (1.9 cm) flats
  series 7800 ⅛-inch (0.3cm)
  and ⅜-inch (1cm) angle brushes
  series 7300 nos. 4, 6, 8 and 10 flats
  series JS nos. 2 and 10/0 liners
  series 795 no. 3 round
  an old, frayed no. 10 flat

- 220-grit sandpaper

- two 1-inch (2.5cm) foam brushes

- MinWax Early American stain

- tracing paper

- transfer paper

- transparent or masking tape

- stylus

- ruler

- waxed palette paper

- palette knife

- DecoArt Brush 'n' Blend Extender

- DecoArt Wood 'n' Resin Gel Stain (optional)

- plastic wrap or plastic bag

- white chalk

- McCloskey's Heirloom Eggshell Varnish

- mineral spirits

- tack cloth

- soft cloths

This pattern may be hand-traced or photocopied for personal use only. Enlarge at 154% on photocopier to return to full size.

Shading markings on the scrolls are just suggestions. It's fun to create variations, so don't feel bound by the strokes indicated here.

This form is created later by shading.

These shapes are created later by shading and highlighting.

1 Prepare the Surface

Before you start your project, think about how you might like to do it differently than I did. I like pretty edges on plain surfaces, so my sweet husband routed the straight-cut top edge of the lazy Susan. I also love the look and feel of natural wood, so when a project lends itself to leaving some of the wood exposed, I take advantage of it. For this reason, I painted part of the design on stained (rather than painted) wood, letting the grain of the wood show through. If your wood does not have a pretty grain—or if the grain is too busy—you may prefer to paint the entire surface. Burnt Umber would be a close match to my stain color. Or you may prefer a different color altogether. (Imagine the entire design painted on a light background.)

Think about the scroll colors as well. It would be a simple matter to change them to match your decor. You simply need to choose a medium value for the scrolls, a dark value for the shading and two lighter values for the highlights. With these decisions made, you're ready to begin.

Sand the surface smooth with 220-grit sandpaper, moving in the direction of the grain. Remove the sanding dust with a tack cloth. Use a 1-inch (2.5cm) foam brush to stain the entire surface. I used MinWax Early American, a soft, warm color like Burnt Umber. This spirit-based product takes longer to dry (four to six hours for the first coat, eight hours for the second) than the acrylic stains (which take about thirty minutes) but I like the deep, rich coloring it provides. If you prefer working with a water-based, quick-drying stain, try DecoArt's Wood 'n Resin Gel Stain in Walnut.

While you're waiting for the stain to dry completely, enlarge the pattern to full size and copy it onto tracing paper. The register mark in the center of the fruit design and the dashed lines will help you center the design and align the repeated parts of your pattern. You will not transfer the entire pattern all at once, so you can trace the scrolls on a separate sheet from the fruit and frame.

This pattern may be hand-traced or photocopied for personal use only.
Enlarge at 115% to return to full size.

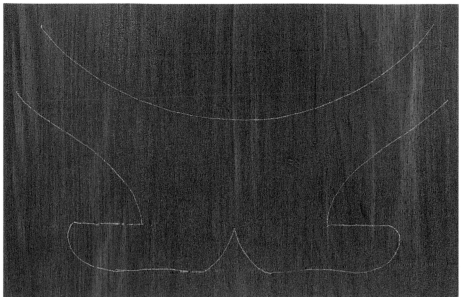

2 Transfer the Frame Pattern

When the stain is thoroughly dry, use the ruler to find the center of your circular project and mark it with a piece of chalk. Move the ruler around the project and measure and mark again two or three times. The exact center should be somewhere in the midst of the chalk marks. Align your traced fruit and frame pattern so the register mark rests in the middle of the chalked area and the dashed line extending vertically below the fruit aligns with the grain of the wood (if you're working on a stained background). Tape the pattern in place and slip a piece of transfer paper under it with the coated side facedown. With a stylus or dried-out ballpoint pen, trace lightly over only the outline pattern lines for the frame (the bold lines on the pattern).

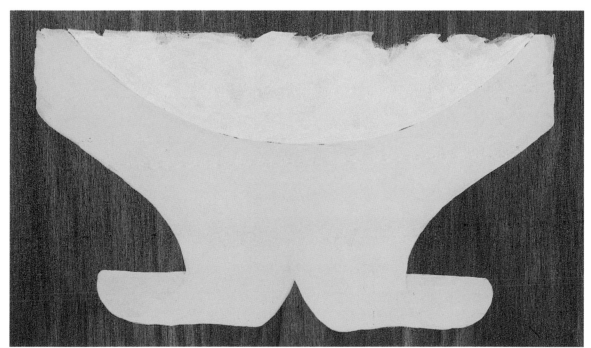

3 Basecoat the Background and Frame

Use a ½-inch (1.3cm) or ¾-inch (1.9cm) flat brush to basecoat the background inside the frame with Toffee. Use short, choppy strokes to create variations in texture and coverage. Apply a second coat if necessary, but don't worry about achieving smooth, even coverage here. Use a ½-inch (1.3cm) flat brush to basecoat the frame with Yellow Ochre. Apply three or more thin coats for smooth, even coverage with no ridges. If your brush deposits a ridge of paint, use your finger to wipe across the ridge and back into the painted area.

4 Marble the Background and Color-wash the Frame

Use the palette knife to mix a juicy puddle of Mocha thinned with water and a little extender. With the ¾-inch (1.9cm) brush, quickly brush the mixture into the center of the background, then spread it out to the edges. While the paint is still wet, gently press a piece of crumpled plastic wrap or a thin plastic bag into it, then lift the plastic off. This will create a marbled texture. Use a damp brush to quickly wipe up any smears of Mocha that might have slipped under the plastic onto the frame. Any stubborn spots can be overpainted with Yellow Ochre. Use the ½-inch (1.3cm) or ¾-inch (1.9cm) flat brush to apply a thin wash of Antique Gold to the frame. Apply a second thin coat if necessary to achieve a rich, translucent gold.

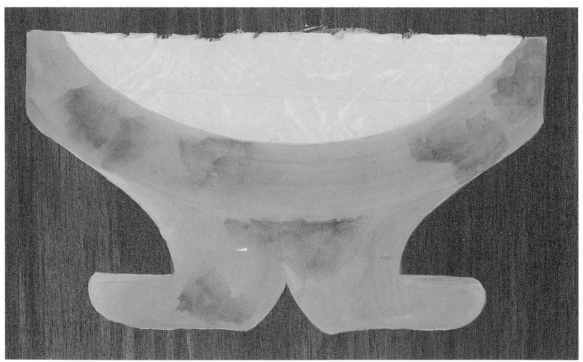

5 Transfer Details and Add Touches of Color

Be sure that all the little puddles in the marble background are thoroughly dry. Then tape the frame and fruit pattern back in place and transfer the fruit, leaves and all the details onto the frame. Lift the pattern to check that the tracing is complete before removing it. Do not transfer the scroll pattern at this time—it would all be rubbed off by the time you finished painting the fruit and frame.

We want to create the look of shiny brass, so we must add colors that would be reflected in the brass from the surrounding fruit and scrolls. The frame is going to look very splotchy at this point, and you will be tempted to overwork it, trying too hard to make things look great. Just relax and have faith that the last step will pull everything together. Dip the ½-inch (1.3cm) flat brush in extender, then sideload it with Country Red. Apply the red in irregular patches around the frame. Use the clean side of the brush to soften strong edges. Repeat this process using Plantation Pine and then Blue Haze (or your medium value scroll color).

6 Shade the Frame

We will float the frame's shading color onto a partially dampened base. The moisture will help disperse the color for an even transition. You will need to work with two brushes: the ½-inch (1.3cm) flat brush and the ⅜-inch (1cm) angle brush. Sideload the long edge of the angle brush with Milk Chocolate. Load the ½-inch (1.3cm) flat brush with water plus a little extender and paint a brushstroke of water/extender along the center of the broad part of the frame (see the large arrow). Try to do about one-fourth to one-third of the frame at a time. While the stroke is wet (but not puddley), shade both sides of it with the sideloaded angle brush, placing the color-loaded side along the inside pattern lines (see small arrows). It's safe to rebrush an area as long as everything is still wet. Once it starts to dry even slightly, leave it alone. After it has completely dried, you can add another layer of thin paint if needed. Paint the smaller ridges on the frame using the same method, applying the water/extender mix from the chisel edge of the brush. Apply two brush-widths of water/extender mix across the centers of the curved handles and shade as before. Paint the narrow, incised lines in each handle with the point of the angle brush. Painting these lines while the handle is still moist (but not puddley) will make them blur slightly, adding to the illusion of depth. To shade the curved, underneath part of the handles, first brush a little water/extender mix on the outside tips, then place the color side of the angle brush toward the inside edge of each handle and pull it down along the curve.

Don't fret about precise edges and blending. Irregularities will give the brass frame character, just as a dented and tarnished antique frame has more charm than a shiny new one.

7 Darken the Shading

If you have anything made of brass, squint your eyes and study it. Notice how intense the darks and lights are. (Also observe what other colors and shapes you see reflected in it.) In order to make our lights vibrant, we must set them against strong darks. Therefore, repeat the process in step six, this time using Dark Chocolate.

8 *Pull It All Together*

This is the step that should make you smile, but you have to promise to walk away after you complete it and enjoy a cup of tea before looking at it too critically. You will work with two brushes: a no. 6 and a no. 10 flat brush. Mix a juicy puddle of Antique Gold, water and a little extender. The mixture should be translucent. Place a little Pineapple in another area on the palette. Sideload the no. 6 flat brush with Pineapple and have it ready. Meanwhile, use the no. 10 flat brush to apply the thinned Antique Gold to the frame, one section at a time. Start with one part of one of the handles, covering everything, even the darkest shading. While the thinned Antique Gold is still wet, brush in the Pineapple highlight, using the clean side of the brush to soften edges into the moist Gold mix. If you lose too much of the highlight, you can add more now or wait until you've completed a first pass over the entire frame with the Antique Gold. When you work on the circular portion, paint only about a third of it at a time so that it stays wet while you add the highlights.

Now go away from the painting for a few minutes. When you return, study the effect. If you need to adjust colors, repeat any of the previous steps in any sequence, always working with thin washes of color. For example, if your reds have totally disappeared, lightly brush them in again. You will notice that your blue splotches have turned green under the gold wash—this will be corrected in step twenty-five.

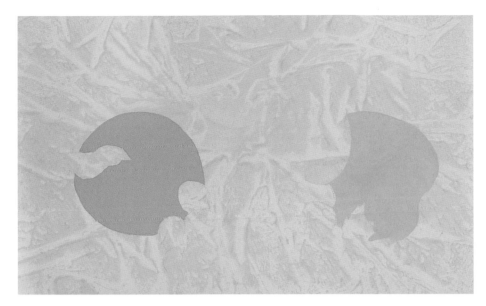

9 *Basecoat the Apples*
Use the no. 10 flat brush to basecoat the red apple with Peaches 'n' Cream. Basecoat the green apple with Hauser Light Green, using the same brush.

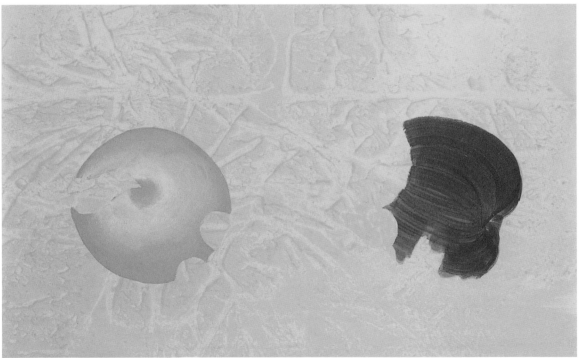

10 *Apply Color Washes*
Load an old, frayed no. 10 flat brush sparingly with thinned Country Red. Follow the contours of the red apple, starting at the stem depression and pulling across the top toward the base. Aim for streaky strokes. Test your technique on your palette to determine how thin your paint must be and how much pressure to put on the brush. Using a good no. 10 flat brush, give the green apple a thin layer of water plus a little extender. Blot the brush slightly, then sideload it with Olive Green. With the clean side of the brush centered in the stem depression, swing a stroke around the depression. Then, flip the brush over so the clean part faces the outside edge and slightly overlaps the previous stroke. Make another swing around the apple. Continue working around the apple, spreading the light wash ever thinner as you approach the edge of the apple.

11 *Shade the Apples*

Make a deep red mixture of Country Red, Cranberry Wine and a little Hauser Medium Green. Cover the red apple with a thin layer of water plus extender. Sideload the no. 10 flat brush with a thin wash of the deep red mix. Apply this wash sparingly in several thin layers, drying thoroughly between each, until the desired depth of shading is reached. Shade the area that will be behind the pear and grapes. Shade the apple stem depression by placing the color side of the brush facing the bottom of the depression and the clean side toward the top of the apple.

Moisten the green apple with a thin layer of water plus extender.

In the area just below the stem depression, brush on a little thinned Cadmium Yellow, using the no. 10 flat brush. Quickly rinse the brush and sideload it with a thin wash of Blue Haze. Shade the lower edge of the apple by placing the clean side of the brush along the bottom of the apple and making a stroke. Then flip the brush so the clean side faces the top of the apple. Make a second stroke barely overlapping the first. Blend a little if necessary. Shade inside the stem depression by placing the color side of the brush toward the top of the depression. Add a pink blush along the upper side of the apple by brushing a thin layer of Raspberry onto the dampened background.

12 *Highlight the Apples*

One apple at a time, moisten the surface with water or extender. Sideload the no. 8 flat brush with Pineapple. Brush the Pineapple into the moisture until a thin veil of light color covers the highlight area. Use the clean side of the brush to soften edges. Load the no. 2 liner brush with thinned Pineapple and scatter tiny dots all over the green apple. Do clusters of six to eight dots at a time and then blot with your finger to soften the dots.

13 Pull It All Together With Shine and Shadow

If you need to unify the colors on the red apple (as we did with the brass frame), use the no. 10 flat brush to apply a thin layer of Country Red or Blush Flesh (a softer tone) over everything. Then use the no. 8 flat brush to lay a strong Pineapple highlight within the highlight area to make a pronounced shine. Unify the colors on the green apple with a thin wash of Light Avocado. Then wash a thin layer of Toffee over the Raspberry color to create the dull "frosting" on the apple. Add the shine with a stroke of Pineapple.

Tip

After all the fruits are completed, you may want to make some minor adjustments to help them relate to one another and to the scroll border. For example, working Blue Haze faintly into the shadows ties the red and green apples together and coordinates them with the scrolls. ❦

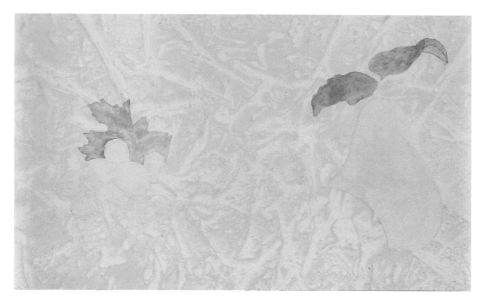

14 Basecoat the Grapes, Pear and Leaves

With the no. 8 flat brush, basecoat all the grapes and the pear with Yellow Ochre. With the same brush, undercoat all the leaves with a thin, puddley wash of Light Avocado. As the wash dries, you should see a variety of lights and darks. This will create more interest in your leaves than an even coat of paint. If the resulting wash is too light, as shown on the grape leaf, repeat the process.

15 Apply the Colorwash

Use the no. 6 flat brush and Raspberry thinned with water to cover all the grapes, letting some appear light, others darker. Use the no. 10 flat brush to apply a thin wash of Antique Gold to the pear. If the color dries too pale, repeat this step, being sure that the lightness of the background color still shines through. You will notice that painting the pear is very similar to layering colors in painting the frame.

Make a dark green wash with a mixture of Hauser Medium Green, Blue Haze, a tiny amount of Cranberry Wine and water. Sideload this mixture onto the no. 6 flat brush. Start on the undersides and turned portions of the leaves and the areas behind the fruits. If the color appears too intense, dilute it slightly before continuing. Brush a stroke along the center vein line and scatter additional strokes at random on all the leaves. If you pull the strokes at an angle from the edge of the leaf toward the center vein, you can create a network of what appear to be smaller veins in the spaces between your strokes. (Note the upper right area of the grape leaf.) Be careful not to overdo this or your leaves will become main characters rather than supporting cast.

16 *Shade the Grapes and Pear and Add Color Accents to Leaves and Basecoat Stems*
Sideload the no. 6 flat brush alternately with Crimson Tide, Cranberry Wine and Black Plum. Brush the colors onto the grapes at random, using the Black Plum in particular to create the darkest shadows and strongest depth in the center of the grapes. Brush over the pear with a layer of water plus a little extender. While the pear is still wet, use a no. 10 flat brush sideloaded with Milk Chocolate to shade the left side and lower section of the pear. Begin at the lower left corner, letting the color fade as you move upward and toward the right. Use the clean side of the brush to merge the color into the water base. Use the no. 2 liner brush and thinned Milk Chocolate to paint the stem depression and to scatter thin freckles over the pear.

Sideload the no. 6 flat brush with thinned Country Red and brush accents of color onto all leaves. Basecoat all stems with Milk Chocolate on the no. 2 liner brush, pulling strokes the length of the stem.

17 *Add Colorwashes to Pears and Grapes, Highlights to Leaves and Shading to Stems*
Sideload the no. 6 flat brush with thinned Peaches ' n' Cream for some of the grapes, and thinned Cadmium Yellow for others. Lay a curved stroke of the light color along the edges of the foremost grapes. The paint should be very thin and make just a subtle change. Brush a layer of water plus extender onto the pear. While the pear is wet, lay washes of color as follows, feathering out the edges with the clean side of the brush: Country Red to the middle right side and bottom, Hauser Light Green to the upper left edge and Blue Haze to the lower left side, creating a somewhat triangular shape.

On all leaves, use the no. 6 flat brush sideloaded with slightly thinned Jade Green to highlight portions at random. In addition, highlight apple and pear leaves with slightly thinned Pineapple. Load the no. 2 liner brush with thinned Olive Green and paint sketchy vein lines, being careful not to add too much distracting detail. Use the liner brush to shade the stems with Dark Chocolate.

18 Add the Final Touches to Grapes, Pears, Leaves and Stems

Sideload the no. 6 flat brush with Summer Lilac. Randomly brush a thin accent highlight on every grape. Then dry-brush a stronger highlight of Pineapple on just a few of the grapes. As you did with the brass frame, unify all the pear colors with a thin wash of Antique Gold. While the pear is wet, brush in Pineapple highlights—thinly at first, then adding a final, strong accent. Mix Pineapple with a little Light Avocado and Milk Chocolate. Use the liner brush to apply the mixture as a highlight on the stem and in the cross-section part of the stem. Brush a unifying wash of Light Avocado over all the leaves. The photo at right shows the finished fruit and leaves.

19 *Transfer the Scroll Patterns*
When positioning the scroll patterns, you may find it helpful to locate the center of the project once again. Do this by rubbing chalk on the back of the fruit tracing just in the area of the register mark. Position the tracing on the painted design and lightly trace over the +. Remove the tracing. Lay a ruler through the + with each end of the ruler extending over the handles of the painted frame. Adjust the ruler until it intersects both handles at the same point. Use chalk to mark a few small lines along, and as close as possible to the edge of, the ruler. These lines will correspond to the dashed lines on your scroll pattern. Repeat the process, this time making sure the ruler crosses the + perpendicularly to the first position. You have now divided the project into fourths. Use the chalked lines to align your scroll patterns. Tape the pattern in place, slip the transfer paper under the pattern and lightly trace over the pattern lines.

 Tips Here are some tips for painting the scrollwork. Most importantly, remember to relax and have fun!

- *Study the pattern for the suggested painting sequence and stroke direction, but please note: The numbers on the strokes are only suggestions, their sole purpose being to get you past the hurdle of wondering where and how to begin. You may actually find it more frustrating trying to align the numbered pattern and your project in order to follow the sequence. If you're comfortable with setting out on your own, by all means do so. It will be a lot more fun.*

- *Generally, I paint the longest, supporting scrolls first, then add the shorter, decorative scrolls.*

- *I almost always paint from the base of the design outward, painting as if a tumble of acanthas leaves is growing as I paint.*

- *Don't try to follow the pattern lines precisely. Doing so will result in stiff, unnatural curves. If your stroke veers from the line, no one will know after you remove the pattern lines. And when you're finished, there will be too many strokes for anyone to try to compare your repeated areas. So relax and have fun!*

- *If I suggest that a segment requires two strokes to complete, and you require three, don't force two. Go for three.*

- *Turn your work to pull strokes in the direction most comfortable for you.*

- *If you get pronounced paint ridges within scroll segments, brush gently over them to flatten the ridges. Otherwise, these ridges may interfere with overlapping elements, as well as with the shading and highlighting.*

- *If you work with too much pressure on the brush, or paint that is too thin or translucent, you may need to add a second coat after the first is thoroughly dry.*

- *If you're selecting your own colors for your scrolls and you plan to antique your project, be sure to choose scroll colors a little brighter than what you want to end up with. The antiquing will dull and deepen the color.* ❦

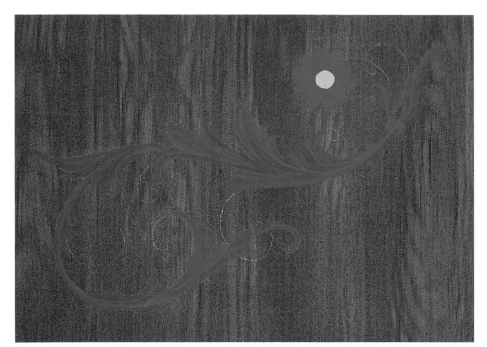

20 *Paint the Scrolls, Flowers and Flower Centers*

Load the no. 3 round brush with Blue Haze (or your medium value color choice). Following the suggestions on page 127, paint all the scroll elements and flowers, leaving the fine lines until later.

Basecoat the flower centers and golden buttons with Yellow Ochre, using the no. 4 flat brush.

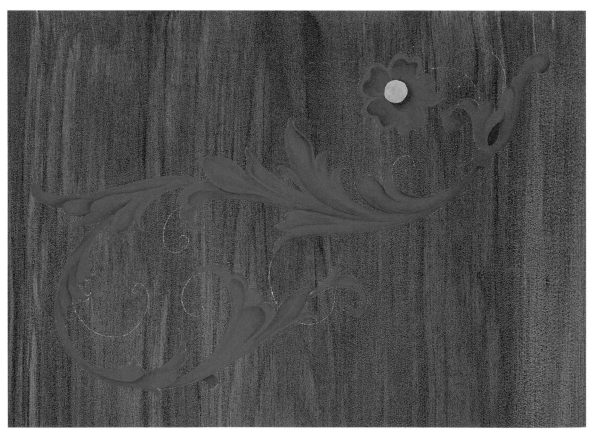

21 *Shade the Scrolls, Flowers and Flower Centers*

Side load the no. 4 flat brush with a half-and-half mixture of Antique Teal and Deep Midnight Blue. Paint shading strokes on the flowers and scrolls to suggest roundness, "underneathness" and "behindness." Watch for subtle variations in color in your basecoated scrolls. They will often suggest where shading could be effective in making interesting fold-over leaf or scroll effects. Don't worry too much about following my painted suggestion. (Besides, another time, I might do the same design quite differently.) Apply a thin wash of Antique Gold to the flower centers and the golden buttons.

22 Highlight the Scrolls, Shade the Flower Centers and Paint the Fine Lines

Side load the no. 4 flat brush with a mixture of Colonial Green plus a little of the Antique Teal and Deep Midnight Blue shading mixture from the previous step. Highlight the lower two petals on the flowers and all the portions of the scroll that you want to appear raised. Use this same mixture and the no. 2 liner brush to paint all the fine line scrolls. Shade the lower one-third of the flower centers and the golden buttons with Milk Chocolate sideloaded on the no. 4 flat brush.

23 *Add the Second Highlight Color*
Use the no. 10/0 liner and Colonial Green to paint distinct highlighting strokes on all the raised forms of the scrolls and flowers. Add an accent dab of shading near the center of each flower center and golden button, using the corner of the no. 4 flat brush sideloaded with Dark Chocolate.

24 Add the Final Touches

Load the no. 10/0 liner brush with Pineapple. Swipe across the top third of the flower centers and golden buttons to create a strong highlight. Rinse the brush and pick up a small amount of Pineapple, greatly thinned. Paint a fine stroke in the lower portion of the flower centers and buttons as a reflected light.

Mix a little Burnt Umber oil paint with enough varnish to make it creamy. Then add mineral spirits until the mixture is almost runny. Load a ⅛-inch (.3cm) angle brush with the mixture and paint the cast shadows. These are fun to experiment with. The further away you place a shadow from the form casting it, the more elevated the form appears.

 Tip When painting cast shadows, I like the transparency of the Burnt Umber oil paint and the way it lets the character of the grain peek through, but you may prefer to substitute Burnt Umber acrylic paint and water for the Burnt Umber oil paint and mineral spirits/varnish mixture. ❧

25 Finish the Project

Study the completed painting to be sure that all the elements coordinate. If any shadings are too weak, intensify them by repeating the shading step. If your leaves are too similar in color, add more reds or blues to some, more yellows to others. Check the reflected colors in the frame; add more if needed, or subdue too strong colors with an Antique Gold wash. Very lightly go over blues that have turned green (due to the gold wash) with a few touches of medium or light-value blue.

Remove pattern lines with an old brush dampened with water. If that doesn't work, try mineral spirits.

After the project has dried for several days—allowing the oil-painted shadows to cure—wipe it with a tack cloth. Then apply two thin coats of varnish. I prefer to use the same type of varnish throughout a project to eliminate the risk of chemical incompatibilities. Therefore, I generally varnish with the same spirit-based varnish I mixed with my oil paint for my cast shadows. I use this same varnish in my antiquing mixture and for my finish coats. If you prefer working with the faster-drying

sprays and acrylic varnishes, test them first to be sure you won't be surprised by unexpected results.

Mix an antiquing glaze using about an inch (2.5cm) of Burnt Umber oil paint and roughly a teaspoon of spirit-based varnish. Mix these together until creamy, then add approximately two to three teaspoons of mineral spirits until the mixture is thin enough to spread easily with a foam brush. Cover the project with the antiquing glaze and let it "rest" for about five minutes, or until the surface starts to appear a bit dull. Then, with a clean, lint-free soft cloth, gently and evenly wipe down the entire project. With a clean area of the cloth, remove more of the glaze from the light background and fruit. The more you rub, the more glaze you will remove. Using a glaze-filled area of the cloth, stipple the light background area to add more texture to the marble background. Keep the darkest shading around the fruit, particularly near the foreground, gradually fading the shading to light as you approach the edge of the frame. Let the antiquing dry for several days, then apply several protective coats of varnish.

About the Artist

Jackie Shaw's love of decorative painting stems from an appreciation of the unfettered enthusiasm—and often naiveté—of the folk painters who created this lively art. In their quest to embellish their surroundings with color and design, a certain joy was infused into their work.

Jackie has immersed herself in that joy for twenty-seven years. She has authored thirty-one how-to books, including *The Big Book of Decorative Painting*, hundreds of magazine articles, seven videos, four TV series, and she has traveled around the world teaching. She's also received the Society of Decorative Painters' highest award, the Silver Palette—given in recognition of efforts to promote decorative painting—and the President's Commendation Award. ❦

Donna Bryant Waterson

PLUMS

This simple, elegant design uses a limited color palette, allowing you to concentrate on value painting while you create fat, juicy plums set beautifully against their own color background. Relying on value to create the look of dimension can present an exciting challenge. This wonderful faux-finished box is perfect for my favorite wild plum herbal tea. 🍂

Materials

- *wooden box available from Valhalla Designs, 343 Twin Pines Drive, Glendale, OR 97442-9766*
- *Accent acrylic paints*
  Teal Deep
  Imperial Antique Gold
  Barn Red
- *Grumbacher MAX oil paints*
  Alizarin Crimson
  Burnt Umber
  Flesh Hue
  French Ultramarine Blue
  Grumbacher Red
  Ivory Black
  Nickel Titanate Yellow
  Titanium White
  Yellow Ochre
- *Brushes*
  Grumbacher series 5100B nos. 8, 10 and 12 brights
  Grumbacher series 5100R nos. 1 and 6 rounds
  Grumbacher Renoir series 727 nos. 8, 10 and 12 filberts
  Accent Golden Elite series 1860 no. 8 flat shader
  2-inch (5.1cm) foam brush
- *Accent Clear Designer Medium Glaze*
- *Grumbacher Quick Dry Alkyd Medium*
- *sandpaper*
- *tracing paper*
- *graphite paper*
- *waxed palette*
- *parchment palette*
- *Grumbacher Brush Soap*
- *plastic wrap*
- *small plastic bowl*
- *stir sticks*
- *Grumbacher Tuffilm Matte Final Finish*

Color Palette

You may want to add a small amount of Grumbacher Quick Dry Alkyd Medium to the color mixtures as you use them. Quick Dry Alkyd Medium will allow the painting to dry to the touch within one to two days. Add about 2 parts medium to 8 parts color mix. Remember to add medium to only the amount of color mix you plan to use in one sitting. Keep the remainder of your color mixtures covered for longer working time.

Mix A = 3 parts Nickel Titanate Yellow + 3 parts Flesh Hue + ½ part Grumbacher Red

Mix B = 3 parts Grumbacher Red + 3 parts Alizarin Crimson + ½ part Burnt Umber

Mix C = 2 parts Alizarin Crimson + 1 part Burnt Umber

Mix D = 1 part French Ultramarine Blue + 1 part Ivory Black + 10 parts Titanium White

Mix E = 1 part Mix A + 1 part Mix B

Color Placement

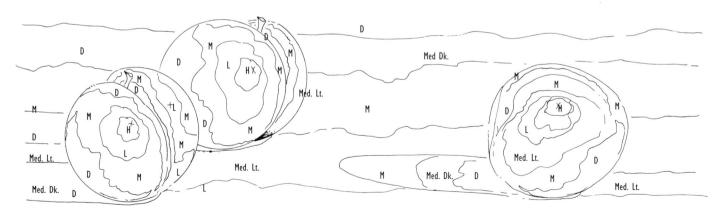

D = Dark Value
Med. Dk. = Medium Dark Value
M = Medium Value
Med. Lt. = Medium Light Value
L = Light Value
H = Highlight

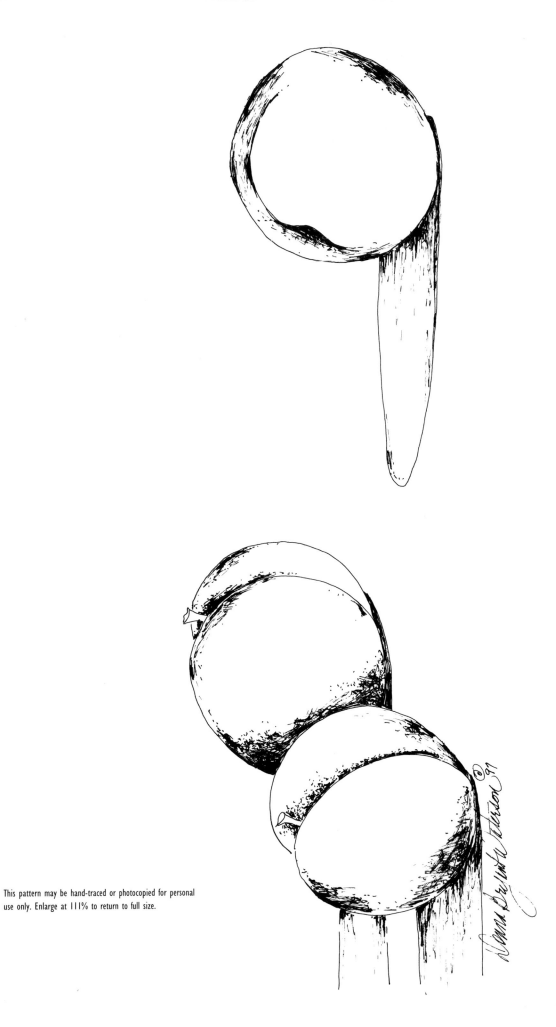

This pattern may be hand-traced or photocopied for personal use only. Enlarge at 111% to return to full size.

1 *Prepare Your Surface*

Sand the wooden surface until it is smooth. Apply two smooth applications of Teal Deep to the box, inside and out, using the 2-inch (5.1cm) foam brush. Allow each application to dry well. Paint the back and sides of the box with the faux technique below. When dry, paint the top rim and knob with the no. 8 flat shader and Imperial Antique Gold. Apply two smooth applications of Barn Red to the lid. Allow to dry well. Mist with Grumbacher Tuffilm Matte Final Finish. Apply the design using white graphite paper.

Faux Technique

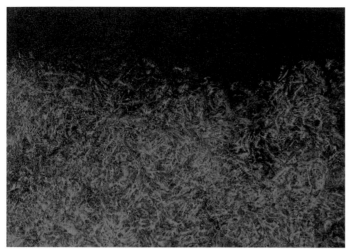

1 Thoroughly mix 1 part Accent Clear Designer Medium Glaze with 1 part water and 1 part Teal Deep. Place some Imperial Antique Gold on the wax palette. Brush the Teal Deep/glaze mixture onto the wooden surface. Apply enough to wet the surface, giving you an extended amount of time to apply and blend the next step. Ball up some plastic wrap in your hand and dip it into the Imperial Antique Gold. Lightly press excess color off onto the wax palette, then tamp the plastic wrap into the wet glaze mix. Lift and blot with an up-and-down motion, rather than with a blending motion.

2 Tamp the gold into the green until you have an all-over textured effect. Allow to dry well.

3 Again mix 1 part glaze to 1 part water. Lightly dampen the surface with this mix, using the foam brush. Load the no. 6 round with Imperial Antique Gold and pressure the round onto the surface to create a random marble vein effect.

4 While the vein is still wet, use a no. 8 sable filbert to soften and mop the vein line into the background. Leave some areas of the vein line strong, some weak. Allow the entire background to dry well.

2 *Block In*
Referring to the color placement chart on page 136, block in the plums using a no. 8 or no. 10 bright. Use Mix B for the medium value areas, Mix C for the dark value areas and Mix E + Mix A for the light value areas.

3 *Blend Values*
Blend the values together using a soft sable filbert brush. Blend enough to soften the values together, but not so much that you lose the slow gradation between values.

4 Add Background

Add the background color using Mix C for the darkest areas, Mix B for the medium value areas and Mix E + Mix A for the light areas. Begin with the darkest areas and work across the top and back of the lid. Move to the medium value as you work in and around the plums. Add the light value as you reach the lower front of the lid. Blend all colors with a soft sable filbert brush. Brighten the light area of the plums using more Mix A. Allow all areas to dry well before proceeding.

5 Add the Shadow Under Plums

Add the shadow under the plums with Mix C. Add a very small amount of paint to the dry surface with a flat brush. Blend and shape the shadow with a filbert brush.

6 Add Splotches, Stem and Frost

Add all additional color to a dry surface, then scrub the color in to blend. Using a small round brush, add splotches of Yellow Ochre thinned with Quick Dry Alkyd Medium. Allow the splotches to dry for a few minutes while you paint the stem. Basecoat the stem with Mix E + a touch of Yellow Ochre. Shade the bottom of the stem and inside the opening with Mix C. Add a small amount of light with Mix A. The soft blue-gray frost is created by adding a small amount of Mix D with a flat or bright brush. Scrub this color into the dry surface here and there, then blend with a soft filbert brush. Brighten the light area again with Mix A plus a small amount of white. Allow all to dry well.

7 Add the Dewdrops

Dewdrops are easy to paint, if you remember one tip: The less paint used, the clearer and brighter the dew drop will appear.

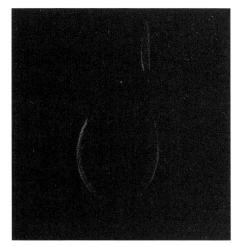

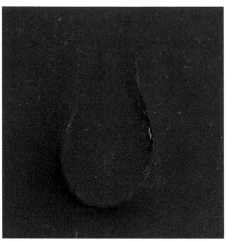

1 Create the shape with a small round brush and Mix A.

2 Shade the underneath area and inside the drop with Mix C.

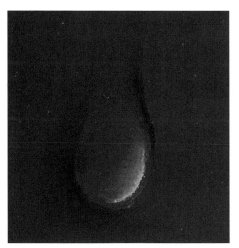

3 Add light with a warm white made by adding a speck of Yellow Ochre to pure white.

4 Add a *life light* using a small round brush and pure, clean white.

About the Artist

Donna Bryant Waterson has been involved in decorative painting and fine art for over twenty-four years. She is a member of the Society of Decorative Painters, the Society of Craft Designers and the Hobby Industries of America. She has served the Society of Decorative Painters as board member at large, treasurer, vice president and president.

She was awarded the SDP's highest award, the Silver Palette, for her contributions to decorative painting.

In addition to serving as Creative Educational Services Manager for KOH-I-NOOR, Inc., Donna has published sixteen instructional books and eight how-to videos on painting and crafting through her own business, Donna Bryant Publications. Her work regularly appears in magazines such as *Decorative Artist's Workbook*, *Decorative Painter*, *Tole World*, *Paint Works* and *Craft Works*. She teaches both nationally and internationally, including in Japan, Australia, Canada, the Netherlands and Argentina. 🍎

Index